To All

DATE DUE

DISCARDED

Demco, Inc. 38-293

Rob Taylor

THE BREACH

Kilimanjaro and the Conquest of Self

The Breach Printing History

1st hardcover edition	*Putnum Publishing Group*	*October*	*1981*
2nd printing	*Putnum Publishing Group*	*November*	*1981*
1st paperback edition	*Kibo Press*	*March*	*1983*
2nd printing	*Kibo Press*	*May*	*1984*
3rd printing	*Kibo Press*	*April*	*1985*
4th printing	*Kibo Press*	*September*	*1986*
5th printing	*Kibo Press*	*March*	*1987*
6th printing	*Kibo Press*	*October*	*1988*
7th printing	*Kibo Press*	*June*	*1989*
8th printing	wildeyes	*July*	*1991*
9th printing	wildeyes	*January*	*1993*

The author gratefully acknowledges permission to quote excerpts from *Coma* by Robin Cook, copyright © 1977 by Robin Cook. By permission of Little, Brown and Company.

Jacket photograph by Rob Taylor
Arrival at the Breach Icicle

Drawings by Melinda Purcell

Rob Taylor also presents *The Breach* as an educational program. For more information contact:

wildeyes
Liberty Ledge
Sudbury, MA 01776
USA
Tel. (508) 443-3021 or (508) 443-3100

Published in the United States of America by wildeyes
ISBN 0-9630188-0-9

In 1978 I returned from Africa with my spirit as much in need of repair as my body. I undertook the writing of my story as a catharsis. In the course of this writing, I came to discover that I had more to tell than a simple narration of events that had come to pass. *The Breach* has been written in the spirit of concern for all who love the mountains and in the spirit of gratitude to all the people who helped me when I was in Africa.

I would like to thank my family for the gift of faith that allowed me to survive the ordeal, the long recovery and the writing of this book. Deepest gratitude to Professor Bill Dowie for his extensive assistance with *The Breach* and for his constant enthusiasm, which buoyed me to persevere and complete the task. Sincere appreciation also to Steve Conroy along with many others who gave in any number of ways suggestions and encouragement.

PHOTO CAPTIONS

1. *Cauliflower ice on the Vettisfoss, a frozen waterfall, in Norway* (ROB TAYLOR)

2. *Ben Nevis in winter—Scottish Highlands* (ROB TAYLOR)

3. *Hamish MacInnes between two gillies (gameskeepers) in a Highland pub* (ROB TAYLOR)

4. *Summit ridge of Djanghi-tau, Central Caucasus, USSR.* (ROB TAYLOR)

5. *Rob Taylor winter climbing in the Canadian Rockies* (JURIS KRISJOHNSONS)

6. *The Diamond Ice Couloir and the twin summits of Mount Kenya* (ROB TAYLOR)

7. *On the summit of Mount Kenya at dusk* (ROB TAYLOR)

8. *The Kilimanjaro National Park rescue team passing through giant heather on Umbwe Route—Mount Kilimanjaro* (ODD ELIASSEN)

9. *Steep ice just below the Breach Icicle—Mount Kilimanjaro* (ROB TAYLOR)

10. *Kilimanjaro panorama—The Breach Wall lies beneath the small circular ice cap left of center* (ODD ELIASSEN)

To Dave
and all my friends
who have died in the mountains

THE BREACH WALL

Tourist Route

Silver Saddle

Window Buttress

Breach Icicle

Shira Plateau

Barranco Bivouac

Umbwe Approach

Moshi

To Marangu

Kilimanjaro from the West

From the surrounding plains of Tanzania, Mount Kilimanjaro rises 19,340 feet to the roof of Africa. On the remote southwest side of the mountain there rises out of the dense green jungles a vast precipitous sweep of volcanic rock, laced by glistening tongues of ice, festooned with immense dangling icicles like giant Swords of Damocles. This, then, is the Breach Wall of Kilimanjaro.

I

Year after year
Life spurns fear
Till the day death has its way

The grimy, somber countenance of the village of Preston molders quietly before him. Now he wonders why he has come. At his feet a thousand blackened chimney pots belch smoke and soot into a sea of haze. He stares at the scene, deep in thought. The grayish discharge momentarily wafts about the smudged eaves and roof peaks, then, caught by the biting westerly wind, streaks upward, vanishing into the leaden March sky. "There will be rain before noon today," he says aloud to no one. "Maybe even snow." He bundles deeper into his large navy-blue duvet to ward off the chill. As he draws in a deep breath his nostrils fill with the acrid, peaty scent of the burning coal. He exhales and once again inhales deeply. It is a smell that rekindles long-forgotten images: wisps of smoke drifting idly upward from the deep, narrow Glenachulich Valley. Once more he sees far below him the rustic highland crofts clinging to sheer, rocky mountain walls. Walls rising steeply to a jagged ridge of snow-capped peaks which ring a tiny village. Into his mind drift fleeting recollections of an earlier, simpler existence, a time when endless winter days were filled by battling up icy mountain flanks with friends to wind-whipped summits encrusted with rime. In the face of the harshest of the North Atlantic gales, the most treacherous of conditions, frost-bite and slab avalanches, they found no climb too severe or dangerous. No mountain corrie or couloir impossible. Youth had a certain invincibility and, along with it, an inexhaustible fitness and a strong, common bond of kinship, which allowed the belief that no obstacle could not be overcome. It was a time of endless winter nights filled with camaraderie and cheer, when one was surrounded by good friends and the warm glow of the pub fires. Grasping their pints of heavy, they recounted and matched lurid tales of the day's successful venture upon the hills. It was a time when death and injury were distant strangers, unrecognizable and unknown quantities out of Southeast Asia reported by John Bryant on radio BBC2.

A tolling from the town below announces the arrival of 9 A.M. The rolling peal reaches up and pulls the figure out of his reverie. The trance broken, vacant staring eyes once more clearly focus down upon the ashen town. He sees Preston now for what it really is, or what man has made it—a damned, ugly eyesore so fouled, so desolate, that trees can no longer survive. It is doomed. He turns his back on the scene. A muted sadness wells up within him and lodges in his throat. It is not sorrow for Preston and its imminent end, but for himself. Perhaps I really should not have come, he muses.

Stiffly he sets off on the cracked and crumbling cement of the angled pathway curving upward round the hillside. He climbs haltingly, with a noticeable limp, favoring his left leg, but soon, after thirty or forty steps, his pace smooths out and the limp becomes all but imperceptible. At the crest of the hill he slows, then falters. Ahead stand two immense oaks, their creased trunks blackened and wizened, losing the near-century of struggle with the chimney pots of Preston. Their naked, arthritic branches stretch skyward, interlocking like a pair of hands pleading for salvation. Between these two trees five small slate steps rise up to two great hewn columns of what was once snow-white granite flecked with black feldspar. He moves slowly forward, step by measured step, then stops abreast of the now pitted and dingy flanks of the columns. His hesitation intimates indecision, perhaps unwillingness to go on. His face darkens. For several minutes he stands framed by the columns, motionless. In three quick steps he passes between the pillars into the cemetery. In all their innocence these are simply three steps. Yet for this man they signify a willing return to a realm he has only glimpsed but knows all too well.

The hill's crown rolls gently away from beneath his feet. The dried brown grass is studded with row upon arched row of gravestones, swirling away in an orderly pattern. Only the varying color, from the crystalline white of the new additions to the hoary coal black of the old, destroys the symmetry. When has death ever been . . . systematic, he wonders. Bed boards of the sleeping eternal.

Angling to the right from the entrance, he heads off determinedly toward the western end of the cemetery. Several minutes' brisk walk and he slows his pace, arriving at the final row of headstones before the decrepit fieldstone boundary. Turning left down the row, he continues with a deliberate heavy-footedness, carefully examining the name on each stone as he passes. Byron. Sloan. Loftess. Williams. Kn . . . owles. "Dave" escapes from him in a barely audible whisper. He stops and mouths the simple inscription on the stone: DAVID AMBROSE KNOWLES, KILLED ON THE EIGER, 13TH OF AUGUST, 1974, AGED 27, SAFE IN THE ARMS OF JESUS. Staring down at the gray, nondescript headstone, darkened and weathered far beyond its age, he smiles weakly to himself. Dave certainly wouldn't care, he never gave a second's notice to appearance. Tears well up in his eyes and soon are streaming down his face. Gently he settles himself down on the raised hump of matted grass at the foot of Dave's grave. Alone, he sits there and cries, on this bleak March day, as he has never cried before. His body is wracked by waves of sobs, he gasps for air, his voice chokes. "Oh, David, why, why does this have to happen?" The names and faces of so many other friends flash before his eyes—Nick, Paul, Dougal, John, Mike, gone forever. "Why can't it be like before? How could those great days have just slipped away forever? David, what changed? How could we have let it? Why didn't we see it coming?" On and on the wailing and the one-sided dialogue continue for some minutes. In the end, tired, with grief exhausted, the figure stiffly stands. Once again staring at Dave's headstone, he understands now there can be no answers here for the living. He feels slightly ashamed at his selfishness. He came today, not so much to grieve for Dave or for his other lost friends, as to grieve for himself.

One year ago, when confronted by death, he fought it, and valiantly. In the end, the conflict wound down in death's favor. He acceded to this fate, accepted his demise. Yet the king of terrors passed him by. Why did *I* survive? he wonders. Glancing around the cemetery now, he is haunted by the image: today, like his friend laid here, he should be buried under one of these gray slates, dead already one year. Somehow, by some act of God or freak of nature, he was spared, given a second chance for life. So rare an opportunity. He would not let it pass unappreciated.

A light freezing rain begins to fall as the figure turns his back upon the gravestones and heads toward the entrance of the cemetery.

II

Off we set across the sea
Two as one
Linked destinies

"Why Kilimanjaro, Rob?" Bill settles back into his black Naugahyde seat, staring blankly across at the British Airways check-in counter inside Logan Airport's cavernous Volpe Terminal.

I shrug. "That's hard to answer." It wouldn't be long before Harley would arrive for our 8:30 flight via London to Nairobi, for he was always punctual. But the wait gave Bill and me a chance to talk. He was always like this, very preoccupied, the nights I left on extended mountain trips. Though we were involved in widely divergent careers—Bill was an English professor and I a mountain climber—I had come to know him well over the past ten years and we had become the best of friends. Perhaps it was because of the differences that a unique rapport developed between us. Tonight as usual he had driven me to Logan, and as usual he grew more inquisitive as the hour of departure approached. He was never personally a party to my varied adventures, but always enjoyed sharing my excitement and anticipation of a new one. For Bill it was not the wonder of peaks that was so alluring but the mystery of why mountains and climbing were so alluring to me. He strove, in questioning me, to unlock their secrets hidden deep within myself.

"Little is known about the southwest side of Kili, called the Breach Wall, but reports from people who have seen it say the face is immense, sheer—and there's a direct approach that is unclimbed."

"So you and Harley want to be the first?"

"I can't speak for Harley, but for me it's not so much being the first as just exploring the unknown."

"Don't they go together?"

"Yes, but they're different sides of the same coin. I don't care about notching first ascents. For me, it's a new land, a new mountain, an unaltered place—without the influence of man. You know, there are fewer and fewer of those places left."

Bill shifts in his chair, taps the tobacco down in his briar pipe and relights it. "I thought one could hike to the top of Kilimanjaro. Didn't a leopard once make it to the summit?" We laugh. The only leopard Bill ever heard of going to the top of Kili was in Hemingway's story.

"If he did, he didn't get there by the Breach Wall. He must have taken the tourist route." Again we laugh, but I explain that there is indeed a way up Kili's great snow dome by means of a gradual hiking trail. "There's a mystery to the place. The natives revere its summit as the House of God—even the tourist route is interesting. But our approach is on the opposite side of the mountain, 180 degrees around. Look at this."

I take from my back pocket a creased, poorly developed photograph. A lake, trees, and some birds occupy the fore-ground. Behind the trees and green mounds are mist and blue sky. Farther up are clouds.

"Well?" asks Bill.

"Look at the top of the clouds."

His eyes dilate with amazement. Rising above the fuzzy puffs is a clear hump of white, sharper in outline than the clouds and with dark patches breaking up the whiteness.

"It's the mountain. It's massive."

"Look to the left." I point to two thin bands of white ice. They point straight up to the great nineteen-thousand-foot sloping dome. We both stare for a moment at the two icicles, like twin tusks of some great animal that serenely guards the mountain's heights.

"It's beautiful," Bill says, wrinkling his brow, "but what do you know about the approach to these icicles, about the jungle, the remoteness, in case something happens?"

"It's the remoteness that I like. Don't you see? That's what is exciting. These days faith in oneself has been replaced by faith in technology. Climbers have come to scaling peaks with half-million-dollar expeditions, tons of equipment and hundreds of men. Harley and I will go to the Breach Wall alone, far from any backup help, cast upon our own resources. For me, that's what climbing is all about. You explore, you do it. You have to depend on yourself."

"And your partner. Right?"

"Right."

"What about Harley? Have you and he climbed before?"

"Yes, but not long routes. That's why we're not going to Kili straightaway. It'd be foolish to try a new route without preparation, anyway. So we'll go to a seventeen-thousand-foot mountain in Kenya first." I decide not to mention that our planned route up the Diamond Ice couloir is something special in itself. A slender channel of ice that rises vertically up the central crevice between Mount Kenya's twin spires, the couloir had been climbed only a handful of times.

"Is Harley good?"

"Probably one of the best rock climbers alive. Not an alpinist, mind you; but there's not a rock formation in existence that he can't devise a technique to scale." I explain that we climbed together on short severe routes like the Vettisfoss in Norway, a frozen waterfall nearly one thousand vertical feet high, its cascade of ice spilled into the air like an immense icicle upheld only by its brittle, frozen shell. It was on this hanging plume of ice, made more fragile by the ceaseless rush of water at its core, that Harley and I learned to respect each other's climbing abilities. He was quick and bold, and he made up for his lack of experience on ice by the confidence and flexibility with which he adapted his rock-trained responses to this new surface. I had always been comfortable on ice. Somehow it was natural to me, and my experience and knowledge of snow conditions and different kinds of ice was a given that both of us could rely on. Our climbing strengths and accustomed mediums complemented each other. Although our personalities were almost opposite, they seemed to mesh like two flywheels in a precision timepiece. "Together I guess you could say we made a good team."

Bill, who has been placidly puffing on his pipe, leans back and blows three quick rings of smoke into the air. "How'd Harley get involved in climbing?"

"Up until he was fifteen, baseball was his whole life. He was a pitcher." I recount the story Harley has told me. How one season the coach didn't start Harley even though he promised him he would. Harley was so upset he just collected his gear and quit the team. Says he hasn't touched a baseball since. He looked for another activity to fill his time and just happened to stumble into rock climbing one weekend when a course was being offered by the White Mountain Club. Harley joined in and immediately liked it, and it liked him. He became very good very quickly.

Bill nods. "But certainly he must have moved on fairly soon from small rock cliffs to mountains." For many climbers this would have been the logical progression; not for Harley.

"He didn't want to be a good rock climber; he would settle for only the best. As with everything he did, when Harley made a commitment to rock climbing, he put his whole being into it." He immersed himself in the sport for months at a time without a day's break, until he and the rock became one. Thousands of climbs in the last ten years have carried him to the far corners of the world. "In twenty-five countries on four continents Harley has mastered the hardest routes, some that were thought impossible to do."

I can see the fascination peaking in Bill's hazel eyes. "How does he afford to climb all the time? Is he rich?"

"Perhaps his family helped him out in earlier days, but now it's different. In the real sense of the word, Harley is a 'professional climber.' That is, he makes his living from his rock climbing." Obviously it was an enviable position to be in, being able to work daily at something you enjoyed as much for leisure.

"But that's impossible. Who'll pay a person to climb rocks?" Bill has confused the simple act of climbing with the results of Harley's climbs; outstanding achievements, bold and daring feats, brought monetary reward.

"Why not? Harley uses his skill as a climber to maintain a highly visible image, a well-known and well-respected reputation. He is in constant demand as a lecturer, as a business consultant, as a rock-climbing instructor." People trust the name Harley Warner; companies know this. That is why over the years Harley has become such a successful rep for a number of climbing-equipment firms.

"You shouldn't get the wrong idea, Bill. Harley doesn't lead a charmed life. He has had to work very hard for success."

"But what is his measure for success? The climb or the cash?"

Like most things, I doubt it could be explained in terms of simply this or that. "I think he realizes success on many levels. Harley's no charlatan. He's a great climber, an artist creating a work of art in his climbing. A climb well done is a source of pride. Why shouldn't he be justly paid for his efforts?"

"I agree wholeheartedly, but, just for the sake of argument, what level of remuneration are you talking about—a Rembrandt or one of Mrs. Tate's three-dollar watercolors?" Bill is digging for something. He won't stop till he finds it.

"I think more toward a Rembrandt. Just yesterday he passed papers on a $150,000 house in Stowe, Vermont. It's beautiful, with a panorama of Mount Mansfield. This January he also incorporated a firm called Peak Pathways to combine and manage his varied interests. Projected earnings are $80,000 this year and he's only twenty-five."

Bill's mouth drops open. It was a common reaction to Harley, someone who had done so much, gone so far, so young. His achievements had a way of making others feel insecure, particularly competitive fellow climbers, who scrutinized every detail of his climbing and personality for weakness or fault. The very traits I sought out in Harley were often the same things construed by others as his flaws. What I saw as strength, drive, and determination, they considered bullheadedness, self-interest, and ruthlessness. The self-assurance and commitment I admired were the conceit and narrow-mindedness they despised. This somewhat controversial reputation seemed the price he must pay for life at the top.

I never felt threatened or insecure in the face of Harley or his reputation, for reputations never impressed me. In fact, most climbers I had shared ropes with never seemed too impressed by their own reputations. People impressed them. And people impressed me by their values, by their actions, not by what others said of them. While I was impressed by Harley's ability on short hauls on rock and by his drive, I knew that my own experience was wider and my knowledge of mountains broader. And I knew the quality of my own determination when I made up my mind on something. I had graduated from a Jesuit high school in three years, despite a response it would be impossible, and I cut through a university bureaucracy to earn my degree outside the classroom. I guess if Harley and I had one personality trait in common it was determination. When we combined our wills in climbing, it seemed we could move mountains as well as climb them.

Out from the gloom of the Volpe Terminal, Harley emerges, striding up to us in a steady determined gait, slightly pigeon-toed. "Hey, man! How ya doin' Rob," he booms in my direction, a loud, flat, nasal voice typically Bostonian. I jump up to greet him, unburdening him of his sacks.

"Good to see you, Harley." I point to the small round roll about his midriff. "I see you've been doing some serious training." We both laugh.

"Yeah, you know how it is when you're climbing and on the road; everyone wants to buy you a pint. I'm climbing well enough, though." Harley has just come off a climbing-sales trip, ranging from Aspen, Colorado, to Freeport, Maine. He looks no worse for the wear, save for the few extra pounds, and Africa will soon take care of that. He spins round and throws out a hand at Bill. "Hi. Harley Warner."

Bill reaches out and clasps his palm, shooting a glance down at the latticework of scars upon the back of Harley's hand. "Hi, Harley. I'm Bill Dowie. I've heard a lot about you!" The strength and firmness of Harley's grip surprise Bill. His skin is as hard and rough as sandpaper.

Harley grins. "I hope it's all been good."

From all sides a reverberating din blasts over the terminal's P.A. system. The woman's crisp British voice echoes back and forth repeatedly off floors, walls, and ceiling—words and phrases many times overlapping each other until barely discernible. I cup a hand to my ear, straining to catch the message.

"That's our first call."

"I've got to phone ABC in New York. I'll meet you upstairs." Harley bounds up the escalator two steps at a time. I watch Bill's bewildered eyes trace his line of ascent up the moving stairs.

"Well what do you think, Bill?"

"About Harley? Well, I can see the go-getter side. I don't think anyone I've ever met has had to go call ABC in New York! Seems personable, but he doesn't fit my picture of what a rock climber should look like, not that I've known any. I just expected someone more . . . athletic-looking." For many people, the stalwart, bullish figure of Harley, with his slight paunch, thinning rust-colored hair, and drooping mustache, seems that of a businessman, certainly not a climber, never mind one of the world's best. Harley always said the essence of climbing comes from within, not from the body. Time and again he proved it climbing cliff faces that far stronger men could not ascend.

"Whatever happened to his hands? All those scars?"

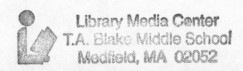

"In the kind of extreme rock climbing Harley does, hands become prime movers, even more so than legs." In the upward struggle against gravity, flesh meets rock, hands battling against razor-sharp crystals, viselike cracks, knife-edged flakes. Even the most cautious of climbers cannot help being cut. "Scarring is the price one must pay for success."

"Your hands aren't like that, though," says Bill.

"An alpinist relies more on his feet and sense of balance than the rock climber who uses his arms and hands." Harley's rock climbing and my mountaineering are about as comparable as surfing and sailing: both are water sports, just as ours are both fields of climbing, but there the similarity ends.

The second call for our flight booms over the P.A. We hurry up the escalator to join Harley in the crush of people at the immigration barricade. While being jostled in line I say my goodbyes to Bill. Our parting handshake goes to an embrace. He wishes, "Have a good trip and a good climb. Be careful."

"Don't worry," I say. "See you next month."

Turning to Harley, Bill takes his hand, "Nice meeting you, Harley. Have a good trip." Then adds, looking to both of us, "Take care of each other."

"Oh, yeh, sure," says Harley, "don't worry, I'll watch out for him."

Harley and I are absorbed by the ebbing masses passing through immigration and security as Bill turns and walks down the long hallway. I watch as he steps onto the escalator and slides downward out of view.

The 747 jumbo jet lifts sluggishly off Runway 9-27 and angles sharply upward over Winthrop and Point Shirley. It fades quickly into the darkness over the wintry seascape of Boston Harbor and the Atlantic Ocean. The blinking red taillight is its last beacon. British Airways Flight 761.

On the right side of the plane in the second no-smoking cabin, Harley and I have three seats between us in which to spread out quite comfortably. In the window seat I cup my hands around my eyes, struggling against the cabin light to look back upon Boston, a myriad of yellow pinpricks of light. One by one they quickly vanish. I watch until the very last one dips into the horizon, much the same as I have every trip over the years since my first one as a boy.

Once the plane is at cruising speed, Harley and I settle into our respective patterns for the long flight across the Atlantic. We knew from our past excursion together to Norway that we had very different responses to travel. For Harley, air flights are synonymous with partying and living it up. Accordingly, on this flight as soon as the bar is open he starts right in with a can of Double Diamond, a light English lager. This he follows with a can or two of Watney's ale, white wine with dinner, and afterward more Double Diamond. The evening wears, but Harley remains as buoyant as ever, apparently unaffected by the alcohol save for the urgent need to get up and offload some of his liquid intake. It's always been the same with Harley; he has an incredible capacity. For me, flying is nothing but a tedium, a quick means of transport, rarely enjoyable, often hassling.

A noticeable lull spreads over the cabin, the passengers all busy with the evening meal. Soon there is only the soft, steady guttural roar of the engines to be heard. I lie back in my seat, head resting on a pillow wedged up against the wall of the cabin, and listen to the continual droning. Here I am suspended in space over the Atlantic, the great divide of water between the known and the unknown. Yesterday I skied the familiar track through the woods around my home. Over the years I have come to know every rock, every tree on the grounds like old acquaintances. Now this jet is hurtling me at the speed of sound toward a continent and countries I know next to nothing about. Tanzania, Dar es Salaam, Arusha—the very names are exotic, opaque, resistant to my Western understanding. The Dark Continent. And the mountain whose southwest side is called the Breach, the most mysterious of all. The hum of the engines is hypnotic, beguiling me into a state of deep, peaceful rumination. My entire body relaxes, every muscle and limb deadening, succumbing to slumber. Yet, another part of me awakens, comes alive. Pictures from the past, thoughts race by, flickering on the interior screen of my mind, a thousand frames a second. Once more I see the small boy before me. It has been so long, I barely recognize him.

A light snow idly sifts down out of the steely blue-gray October sky. It is not one of those hazy, socked-in skies with no visibility, but one with the overcast so high the purplish clouds seem on the very edge of space, much higher than any of those honking V formations of birds migrating south could ever fly, even higher than that jet plane streaking westward overhead. Its silvery tail spins a slender thread of white that slashes the heavens in half from horizon to horizon, yet still it is well below these clouds. Staring upward, the small boy shivers from the cold fall air as he thinks of Mr. Wilson's words, "Ya see those clouds? Today we're gonna go up and touch 'em." To the boy these words are incomprehensible, terrifying, calling up within him images of deadly dangers and horrifying drops at his heels. Yet in spite of his fear, his misgivings, something draws him on, compels him.

The square brown trailhead marker is engraved with white letters:

MT. OSCEOLA
4,536 FEET
3.75 MILES TO SUMMIT

Silently the boy sets out with his group. At first he instinctively hugs the heels of Mr. Wilson, matching his every movement step for step, eyes cast downward, seeing nothing but the soles of his guide's old Dunham hiking boots and the path immediately below. Hours pass. The group slowly gains altitude, and the small boy falls back from Mr. Wilson's heels. The trail, switchbacking its way upward, holds many wonders. The boy moves forward eagerly, totally immersed in this fantastic, alien realm, absorbed by the continual uphill exertion, eyes open wide, mind and body responsive to everything. There is no room now in this small body for apprehension. The fear and anguish that gripped him this morning at the start now dissipates, then vanishes entirely.

Ahead, the trail is carpeted with a thick mat of fallen leaves as it tunnels forward beneath a vast canopy of sugar maples, scarlets, russets, golds, and oranges. The colors are like nothing the small boy has seen before. Bewildered, he spins in circles, gazing wildly about, trying to take it all in. Later, and higher up, he passes through a grove of poplars enrobed in shimmering gold. He is struck by their rich, pure, concentrated yellowness. Yet he wonders why the birches are so similar in color and the maples so varied and multicolored.

Caught up in the rhythmic motion of hiking, the small boy scarcely notices the gradual change from deciduous zone to Canadian zone and the constant drop in temperature. It is, in fact, the change in the trail he notices first. It becomes steeper, full of round boulders and shards of rock and water. Water seems to be everywhere. The trail itself becomes a small brook. Just managing to keep his feet dry over a particularly boggy section, he pauses at the trail's edge and looks up. For the first time he sees the transformation. Gone are all the dappled colors. The world is now carpeted by an infinite number of emerald shades, larches, hemlocks, firs, and spruces, all swathed in layers of lichen and mosses. Onward and upward he moves, each step bringing new sights, new experiences, new adventure.

Soon the angle eases. The surrounding conifers are now dwarfed and stunted into bent configurations. Light snow starts as the group rushes ahead, anticipating the approaching summit. The small boy moves along in their midst, excited but feeling something more. He cannot identify it. He is amazed it can be cold enough to snow, yet he is so hot. His shirt and sweatshirt are soaked with perspiration. Suddenly the group breaks out of the trees. There is nothing now before them. Nothing but a few angled slabs of rock leading up to a giant mound of stones, a cairn marking the summit. The group breaks into a run the last few yards, racing one another to the cairn and climbing up onto it. The small boy is tired and slightly winded from the exertion. It has been a long 3.75 uphill miles, longer than anything he has ever done before. Yet he has made it and he is pleased.

Sitting at the base of the cairn, he is puzzled. The summit is not at all as he imagined or feared it would be. He pictured a mere pinpoint of rock piercing the sky, affording views in every direction. It is instead a broad, flat bump offering views of nothing but sky. He is, deep down inside, a little disappointed.

Shouts from beyond the summit bring him to his feet, and he heads in that direction. The small boy, padding carelessly down the gently inclined rock slab, suddenly turns to stone in his tracks. There he stares, mouth open, at the scene. Fifteen feet before him into an abyss, the cliffs of the Osceola East Face drop sheerly away, two thousand feet down to the valley floor. Several of the guardians and boys sit on the edge, dangling their legs over the void, beckoning him to join them. But he stands paralyzed, motionless, unable to take a single step forward, unable to take a single step backward. How can they sit there, he wonders, so close to the edge? Aren't they afraid? From within him a dizzying fear of heights, of falling, wells up so powerfully he can taste it, as adrenalin surges through his body. He feels his racing heartbeat pounding in his temples as he shivers uncontrollably. And yet, yet, this is the most beautiful thing the small boy has ever seen. It must be as a soaring hawk surveys the world. It is fantastic and so high. Unbelievable! The forests are no longer forests now but immense colored carpets where individual trees are the threads in the pile. It is a carpet upon which no man can walk, and the lakes and ponds are now but silvery hand mirrors that will reflect no man's image. He wonders if perhaps God uses them. At once now he is torn by a war of conflicting emotions: a sense of power at having all the world spread at his feet, yet utter powerlessness. He is like a flea upon some huge animal's back. It is so immense, so far down. A slip or false step spells certain death.

"Hey, Tom, give it back. Mr. Chandler, Tom's going to throw my hat off."

"Cry baby!"

"Okay, guys, the two of you knock it off. Hey, don't you wanna come over here?"

The small boy cautiously lowers himself down to sit on the ground now that he has adjusted somewhat to the exposure. Although he feels there is some part of him that so much does want to go to the edge, he dares not approach any closer now. Admiring the view from this safe spot, he still cannot fathom how he could be so happy, feel such enjoyment, and yet at the same time be so shaken, feel such apprehension. To be wracked by such feelings is very troublesome; he wonders what it all means. Silent contemplation brings him no resolve. The lure of the edge proves too much. Before long he gives in. He creeps slowly forward on all fours, inch by inch, each move receiving his utmost concentration. Those last fifteen feet totally absorb him. So much so that everything else around him ceases to exist. There is only his slow-paced motion, the rock surface immediately ahead, and within him the struggle of his feelings to go on or not to go on. The challenge is invisible. It lies not on the ground before him but deep within. Nearing the edge, he falters, frozen with fear. He does not think he can go on. For a second he doubts that he can win the battle against the unseen terror. But steadfastly he holds, motionless, several minutes until the wave of fear passes. Two more crouched paces and he drops himself down flat to lie prone on the rock surface. Trembling, he peeps uneasily over the edge. With nothing now but two thousand feet of air between him and the valley floor, he exclaims, "Oh! I've done it. Fantastic. I've made it." His words have more to do with himself than with the view. Never in his life has he ever felt such accomplishment, such exhilaration as if he were flying, such terror as if any second he were about to fall.

"Look down there," one of the boys shouts. "You can see a red station wagon on the road. It's a fire car."

"Hey," Tom yells down the chasm of air, "where's the fire?" Everyone laughs.

"Say, isn't that the road we came in on?"

"Naw, you could never see it."

After several minutes in this position, the small boy carefully draws himself up, self-satisfied, and backs on all fours away from the edge. After several yards he stops at what he deems a safe place and sits down. As he gazes out upon wave after wave of majestic mountain peaks and ridges, his spirit soars. They appear infinite in number, stretching on to eternity.

"Come on, boys, let's go. Time to head down." The yells of Mr. Wilson shatter his tranquility. He is sad. Once more his spirit is earthbound. One last look at the peaks and he turns back. Oh, how he wishes he could spend his entire life climbing, roaming these mountain flanks, coming to know every one of them. At the summit cairn he joins the rest of the group. The novelty of the mountain trip has worn off for most now. They are bored, anxious for the journey down. The small boy cannot understand why they do not share the feelings he has discovered today.

The wind picks up in the course of the descent, the weather gradually worsening to a steady snow. But the small boy is oblivious to the biting cold and the whitening ground, oblivious even to his own walking. While the rest of the group run about, chasing each other, playing tag, chatting about what they'll have for dinner back at camp, he is deep in thought, trying to resolve the many questions that have been raised in him today and that he himself has raised. What was special about mountains? Something, but what? Why did he feel toward them the way he did? So different from the way he felt about, say, a pond, a meadow, or a forest? He tries to recall the sensations he had on the summit. Elusive memories now. How could a thing unleash such emotion? What book may have the answers?

By the trail's end he has evolved his own ideas and feels satisfied with the answers he has arrived at. Man is really comprised of two parts: a body, which is material, set upon the earth as a solid, and a spirit, which is an invisible substance like a soul inside the body. Bound together, they make up a man. Mountains are special places that spirits love, places where somehow they can, for a short time, be released and set free. The only way they can get to the mountains is through bodies, since spirits can't move by themselves. Spirits can be hurt but, because they are infinite, can never die, whereas bodies are finite and all must die someday. For the body, mountains are fearful places holding mortal dangers. The strange conflicting feelings one has simultaneously in high places are the body and the spirit disagreeing, quarreling. As the small boy saw it, to climb, an individual must develop a keen sense of self, of each part—body and spirit—binding them into a partnership, letting neither dominate. To the small boy it was incredible—suddenly to think of mountain climbing as so much more than just climbing a mountain. With the sights and feelings of the day's outing still vivid in his mind, he succumbed to the lure and enticement of the mountains. Their images stirred his body and soul, fired his imagination. He was their captive.

From that day forward I, as that small boy, resolved to spend, as best I could, the remainder of my life in the mountains. Coming to know them, learning their secrets, and through them knowing myself better.

With time, I came to know those very same peaks I had seen as a small boy, the White Mountains of New Hampshire, appearing to me then infinite in number, stretching on to eternity. Later I found that their number was in reality less than fifty. In the years that followed I made their acquaintance, some by easy hiking paths, others by sheer faces. I discovered that each of these newfound friends had a special character and identity, whether it was the hulking, brooding mass of Mount Moosilauke, the round, wind-swept dome of Mount Pleasant, or the pointed rocky spire of Mount Chocorua. Each was unique. And yet, each time I toiled and scrambled upon their flanks, there returned the same feelings and emotions that had been aroused that very first day as a small boy on Mount Osceola.

Freed by mountains, my spirit soared ever higher above the ranges in joy, held aloft by the wonders they showed me. Yet ever alert did I keep my mind, for the safety of my body, never allowing it to be overwhelmed, never intoxicated by the mountain's irresistible lure and beauty. With time the shivering, blinding fear of my youth became reverence and respect for all that one encounters in high places. The crumbling ridge of rock, the howling blizzard fast approaching, the deep-blue crevasse lurking beneath the snow-covered glacier, all demand utmost clear thinking and decisive action. Only restraint, vigilance, and agility separate a life of continued happiness from one of perpetual remorse. The great rewards of the mountains necessitate and justify great risks.

The clatter of trays snaps me out of my musings. Dinner is finished. Turning over, I am just in time to see Harley flag a harried blond flight attendant on tray-removal duty. He wants a Double Diamond. I watch her face, strained and perspiring, as a hint of incivility ripples across it. It is just for a second, then she reconsiders. Grabbing his five-dollar bill, she rolls quickly away, reappearing in a moment with the can and change.

"Thanks, sorry for the trouble," he says curtly to empty space as she dashes down the aisle to resume her work. Harley, looking across and seeing that I am watching, whispers, "Did you see that? For a second I thought she was going to haul off and belt me. Just because I wanted a beer."

I only nod, then turn back to my previous position. The deep rumble of the engines soon soothes me back into restful contemplation . . . but Harley continues to monopolize my thoughts.

Who is this person sitting only three feet away from me? This person who, over the next weeks, I shall rely on body and soul? Although we sit side by side, he is a stranger to me still. We share so little besides our climbing.

The Vettisfoss flashes to mind. That March morning, Harley and I had started on the waterfall before first light. The frozen cascade reared up before us into the still-dark sky. I moved upward, driving in ice axes and crampons, snaking an erratic route through the jumbled chaos of ice. At intervals of thirty feet I would stop and place an ice piton, securing the climbing rope to it, then continue on. This was the sole means of protection should a slip or fall come. The rope trailed away from my waist down to Harley, who belayed, paying out slack and attentively watching me for any difficulty. When the rope began to grow taut between us, I would stop at a ledge; then he would climb up to join me and take over the lead. In this fashion we leapfrogged upward, 150 feet at a time.

By afternoon we had ascended seven hundred feet of the waterfall's nearly one-thousand-foot length, arriving at what proved to be the climb's crux, a slender column of grotesque ice, its surface knobbed and convoluted, brittle icicles clinging everywhere. Our route would take us onto and straight up this pillar whose steepness and overhangs looked tougher than anything below. We held a brief strategy session. With these short Norwegian winter days it would be dark in two hours, three at the most. Could we make it to the top by then? Should we stop? Retreat? We both agreed it was best to go for it. We climbed on, still alternating the lead. The ice ahead hung dangerously over us like a fragile lace curtain. It made for slow, tedious, cautious going. Many times, because of the angle, there were no ledges at all. To rest, we were forced to drive in ice screws and hang from our waist belts, the harness cutting into us, squeezing off blood flow. The hours passed unnoticed, afternoon changing to twilight to dusk. As much as we had hurried, we were benighted still a hundred feet from the top. Fortunately, almost as soon as it had grown too dark to see, a moon rose. In its light, reflecting off the ice surface, we pushed on. Finally at 8 P.M. there was only star-filled sky before us. We stood on top and shook hands. Our teamwork that day, a near-perfect synchronism of movement and attention, had allowed us success.

Still I know that for success, even for survival itself, on an immense mountain wall as remote and isolated as Kilimanjaro's Breach Wall, it will take more than climbing compatibility. It will take a very special kinship between the two climbers. Not friendship, which the mountain could undermine, weaken under severe stress. Joined by more than simply a fifty-meter Perlon climbing rope, the two will need to be bonded into a working union, each having absolute trust in and reliance on the other, with responsibility to and for each other. United in a brother-hood of the rope rather than a friendship of it, Harley and I would become one, think as one, move as one, the climbing rope becoming our lifeline, an unbreakable link between us. Is this possible for Harley and me? I told Bill that Harley and I were opposite personalities. Could this be more of a problem than I have been willing to admit?

I drift back in time, searching the folds of my memory for a clue, some answer.

III

When did we meet?
Was it winter?
Was it fall?

From the start Harley and I were never friends, hardly even acquaintances though we lived a mere forty miles apart. Differences in upbringing and life-style probably separated us as much as anything else. Harley was born and brought up in the exclusive community of Wildwood. His father, a corporate executive, and mother, an active socialite, instilled in Harley at a young age the advantage of ambition. Early on he accepted the dogma of the dollar. To dream the American Dream was not enough. One had to live it. Thus, from the start, Harley had incredible drive, was successful in anything he seriously undertook. He often said that he could achieve anything he wanted to badly enough. He believed it and usually proved it. An example: As an adolescent Harley had gone on holiday to Britain with his parents, they paying his way. Before leaving the United States he had assured them that he would reimburse them after the trip for his plane ticket. Once in Britain, Harley left his parents and began visiting a great number of small crags and outcrops scattered throughout the country. At each area he climbed, he made certain someone took photographs of him. He rejoined his parents after several weeks and returned home to the United States. Almost immediately Harley began a lecture tour entitled "Harley Warner: Rock Climbing in Britain," at fifty dollars a show. Within months he repaid in full the amount he had promised his parents he would.

I was brought up in Sudbury, Massachusetts, only a few miles from Thoreau's cabin on Walden Pond. During the land-cheap thirties my grandfather had bought 120 acres of marsh and woods, and gradually, over the years, began clearing them for a summer place. In 1954, when I was born, the lodge was winterized and the entire clan moved from the city to begin a small farm. With chickens, pigs, cows and a large vegetable garden to tend, we all had our fair share of chores, as well as the special projects my grandfather envisioned, such as turning boggy swampland into a three-acre trout pond. The grandmother my memory recalls of those early years was a whirling dervish of constant motion, forever pickling, canning, and preserving.

Our nearest neighbors were miles away, so my brother, Mark, and my sister, Chris, became playmates as well as fellow farm workers. Together we roamed the fields and woods in all seasons, exploring. Later, with field guide in hand, I learned about the various trees, birds, and animals that surrounded me. The outdoors was a source of constant fascination, my playground and classroom.

With the self-sufficiency of our rural life we didn't need much money. As a child, I often wondered about this seemingly crazy pursuit of dollars so important to those outside my world. In my family it never became an issue; my mother impressed upon us at an early age that money would not supply us with the things most important in life.

When I finished high school I enrolled in college, but, much to the disappointment of my family, I left after one semester. From the first, I got the impression of professors beyond their rightful bounds, acting as though every facet of life could be analyzed and explained in simple concrete terms. A compulsion to "know it" demanded that everything be taken apart bit by bit, like a frog dissected in a biology class to discover its mystery of life. The compulsion to "prove it" demanded that everything be duly unraveled, like a baseball's innards, as if to discover its secret of flight. I did not care to analyze and pick apart every minutest notion. I believed that to know something was not to prove it but to accede to it, to experience it from start to middle to finish. This world of academia was not for me. The values of my teachers, the values of my classmates, the values leading to high-paying jobs in large corporations not only failed to appeal to me, they repelled me. Many of my friends found a sense of assurance and personal fulfillment in their regular jobs, but I found routine stifling rather than comforting. I always felt locked in when fulfilling the goals of others rather than my own.

As the years passed I came to find that only in the mountains could I be truly happy. And so I gave myself over to them. Not as a hobby or a sport, as golf or sailing is for some weekend enthusiasts. No, not as a mere pastime, but as a way of life—and one without laborious, forced drudgery. I realized early on that my chosen field would never bring financial security. Often I could barely make ends meet. Still, money came second to doing something I enjoyed. I would not let money lead me into a life of quiet desperation like so many in the quest of the elusive American Dream. Mountains were my reality, mountain life the passion which inspired my searching soul.

Harley and I were surely different, yet this was nowhere more apparent than in our development as climbers and our subsequent approaches to climbing. The climbing world is a small one where everyone knows of everyone else. Harley and I had traveled radically divergent paths, so much so that although we had heard each other's name many times over a seven-year period, we rarely met. Only one year ago had our paths finally crossed and we climbed together for the first time. For Harley, climbing, from the very beginning, meant only one thing, technical rock climbing: in essence, the series of actions, moves, and gymnastic techniques which, when linked together, allowed one to move up a sheer and improbable-looking blank wall of rock using only one's hands and feet. These rock faces varied anywhere from thirty feet to well over a thousand, but the final objective and the strict rules of ethics were the same. The rope, pitons, and various rock nuts used in the climb were never to be pulled upon or used for progress. They existed only as a safety backup in the event of a fall. Right from the start Harley discovered he had a special knack, a unique capacity for this type of climbing, whether jamming fingertips and toetips into a thumb-width fissure or delicately balancing up a smooth 70-degree slab of granite. Extreme routes that usually took years of practice to accomplish he had managed almost immediately. He found an activity he could truly excel at, excel beyond his wildest dreams, and, most of all, he loved it. Then and there he made the decision that rock climbing was to be his life's work. His ambition: to become the greatest rock climber in the world.

Dropping out of school to devote his full time to his climbing, Harley spent hours each day practicing on small boulders, crags, bridge abutments, anything climbable. Continuously he improved and refined his style, and soon he was even developing new techniques to overcome obstacles heretofore thought impossible. Within two years Harley made people sit up and take notice as he pioneered many new routes of extreme severity, pushing the boundaries of difficulty into a new realm. Many times he even climbed without a belay or a safety rope to exhibit his remarkable confidence and skill. By his second year of climbing Harley was a worldwide sensation, a phenomenon that could be likened only to a shining star. Anxiously the climbing world waited with bated breath for the next nigh-impossible achievement of heavenly Harley. Harley waxed in the limelight, and the fame only made him push harder. He traveled the world climbing, carefully nurturing his reputation and considerable exploits into a highly visible image. Before long, Harley had developed "Harley Warner" into a comfortable and successful business. Unfortunately, as is often the case with human heavenly bodies, his glow was more meteoric than celestial. Even as he aged a single year, his body shape changed, the natural transition from boy to man. Harley's brilliance began to dim. He gained more weight and lost the magical, mystical something that gave him the edge above all the rest in the world. Already now, younger climbers were surpassing him. He could not hope to compete with them. Thus, to preserve himself and to preserve "Harley Warner," he changed course and headed out into a larger realm, the world of alpinism, in search of new marvels. He entered the world of winter climbing, the world of ice climbing, the world of mountains. It was here, then, that Harley's and my paths crossed. He had just completed a number of ice routes in Colorado. I had returned from the Alps and recently been winter climbing in the Canadian Rockies and teaching ice climbing. Each lacking a partner, we joined together for a trip to Norway, climbing frozen waterfalls.

In my life there had never been a definite point separating or differentiating my mountain climbing as defined in "hiking" and my mountain climbing as defined in "alpinism" or technical alpine climbing. For me the transition was a simple matter of progression: walking on level ground, hiking uphill, scrambling, and technical climbing—that is, climbing with a rope, where a fall could be fatal. Each was related, yet I felt that each was an enjoyable, worthwhile and satisfying activity unto itself, no better, no worse than the one that preceded or followed it. Harley's love for rock climbing was not matched by a love of hiking. The exhilaration he felt in climbing a route no one else could do, on the edge of danger, at the center of public attention—he could not find these things in walking. For Harley, hiking was a necessary chore for getting to and from climbing.

In my love of the mountains, in my pursuit to know them and understand them better, roped climbing came to me solely as a means of protection in the airy, sublime places I sought to enter, on the spired pinnacles I began to scale. These held mortal dangers in the event of a slip, and the security of the rope was a necessary safeguard. Whenever possible in those days of early adolescence I went climbing with ice ax and crampons in the glacial ravines and corries of Mount Washington and amidst the other mountains of northern New England and Canada. Thus it was that alpinism allowed me to penetrate safely and to glimpse the very essence that was mountains. This technical climbing brought its own unique satisfactions.

Mountains pose continual questions for the alpinist: the dripping verglas chimney rearing upward overhead into a deep black slot, the steep bristling bulge of blue ice, hard as plate glass, barring further progress above. These are the unknown challenges the mountains present to the climber. Their variety and character are limitless as the imagination. No two alike. Yet, unique as every passage is, each requires a similar procedure for success. Like a puzzle, the mountain waits to have its secrets unlocked. The alpinist sizes up the obstacle before him: How shall I approach this, left or right? Where can I rest? Are there enough handholds? Scrutinizing its countenance, he searches out the hidden facets and weaknesses it may hold. Once decided upon a plan of action, he sets off upward. His climbing is a series of linked fluid motions.

Whether it is the ice ax driven high above into the merest dimpled weakness in the bulge or the gloved hand wedged securely into a slender granite slit, each movement is purposeful, efficient, that which best suits the intricacies of the problem the alpinist is surmounting. Cramponed feet searchingly, gingerly scratch millimeter footholds into the glistening, slippery surface. Higher and higher he precariously inches, using finesse, proper technique, and a keen sense of balance. Soon the riddle is solved. The chimney or bulge is overcome. The successful resolution of such a confrontation, man versus element, holds its own gratification for the climber. But as I found from that first day as a small boy, these were secondary in comparison to the fruits of the battle of the spirit. Alpinism causes great uncertainties: Will we make it? What about this lightning storm or that tottering serac wall? Can we survive the roaring avalanches and rockfall? Will I be alive tomorrow? Uncertainties bring to the surface anxieties that usually lie submerged deep within oneself. Facing these tumults of mind and spirit, and eventually surmounting them, has always provided me with a great challenge and sense of self.

Truly this was one of the great attractions of alpinism for me, along with the pure physical pleasure I found simply in the movement of climbing well. Like the precise, well-practiced movement of the ballerina, smooth, graceful, elegant, drawing all eyes to the stage, so, too, did I see the dance of the alpinist, flowing beautifully, demanding perfection, yet performed in the mountains, carried out in a realm of sublime remoteness for the satisfaction and happiness of the climber alone, and perhaps God's. The ballerina, one with the music; the alpinist, one with the mountain. Thus the integral gestures of alpinism, those progressive movements joined fluidly together, became sufficient unto themselves to elicit ecstacy. The binding confines of the climbing rope opened a limitless world of freedom. Yet freedom without knowledge could be deadly, especially in the mountains. I realized I must somehow acquire the skills and expertise to live and work in the mountains. In 1972 at seventeen years of age I left America for Scotland.

IV

In the halls of learned men
I read the writing on the wall

The Highland omnibus ground uphill in first gear, weaving through the narrow steep Glencoe Gorge in the half-light of dusk. In only minutes now my journey would be over—that is, if I was to believe this Hamish MacInnes' letter. Who knew, though? Thus far my trip had gone little by plan. It had taken three days to negotiate the 120 miles between Glasgow and Glencoe with poor hitchhiking, missed busses, wrong routing. By the end of my second day I had ended up on the seacoast, at the fishing town of Oban, instead of in the Highlands. That night, lying in one of the bunks at the fishermen's mission, I stared sleeplessly at the ceiling, thinking about what had brought me to the homeland of my ancestors. I sought not the long-lost heritage of the clan Taylor but secrets of a different sort within the Highland hills, the birthplace of modern alpinism. Though the sport of mountain climbing—climbing to vanquish summits—had originated in the Alps, here in Scotland the idea of climbing for the challenge of self, for the sheer enjoyment, was born. Bell, Collie, Slingsby—they were the pioneers of Scottish winter climbing. For them, conquest of peaks meant nothing, the mountain experience everything. It was a tradition still carried on today in the Highlands by Hamish MacInnes and a host of others. For this reason I found myself over three thousand miles from home, wandering the Scottish hills.

I dropped down to the asphalt, the door slamming behind me, and off sped the bus. This couldn't be right, I thought. The expanse of moor stretched away as far as the eye could see—to distant snow-capped peaks—treeless, featureless, unbroken save for two low-slung whitewashed cottages beside me. The wild desolation of the place was disconcerting.

Across the moor two figures fast approached. Once beside me they silently looked me up and down, and I them. Water oozed from their worn creased climbing boots. They wore belts cinched round their waists, with stubby ice axes holstered on each side, as a quick-draw gunslinger would wear a pair of Colt .45s. Mud and grime splattered their breeches and anoraks, worn on a thousand mountain trips.

At last the shorter, slighter one with the drooping mustache spoke. "Unh-huh? You've certainly taken your time getting here, Robbie isn't it? I hope this isn't an indication of your performance on the hill." Not waiting for a reply, he brushed past, adding, "We'll see tomorrow. Be ready half seven. Come on, Ian, time for a pint."

The big one, Ian Nicholson, smiled, a soggy cigarette clenched between his teeth. "Don't mind Dave," he said, voice thick with Scottish burr. "He got stuck with some real puntas today—from Cornwall. Never saw snow before." He heaves a great laugh which dissolves into a hacking cough, and moves on. "Tomorrow, then, Robbie."

The following days I climbed with Big Ian and Dave Knowles. I held my own with them on the approaches, the climbing, and the descents. Initially they were surprised that a foreign lad could climb so well so young, as if this were the domain only of true Scots. I was impressed by their uncanny ability on "mixed" ground, terrain that is not all ice nor all rock, but a hodgepodge of the two. It was a prevalent condition on Scottish routes and a medium they had mastered. By week's end suspicions between us had been replaced by mutual respect, and I sensed the start of long friendships with Dave and Ian.

My meeting and subsequent friendship with Hamish Mac-
Innes proved just as serendipitous. As I hitched through the glen
one afternoon, he stopped to give me a lift. He looked just like the
dozens of pictures I'd seen of him, tall, willowy, with ginger hair
and scraggly gray beard. Before I opened my mouth he ex-
claimed, "Och aye, you must be the American." We raced away
in his souped-up mini-van, the G forces pressing me back into my
seat. This day he surely proved true the rumor of his penchant
for hot cars and fast driving. The mini hit top speed. White-
knuckled hands firmly gripping the vibrating wheel, eyes locked
on the road, he rattled on about no end of subjects: the lack of
rain in the southwest, Beverly Sills's performance in *Manon*,
hang-gliding in California, the use of heated blood plasma in
reviving hypothermia victims, even climbing. As he slowed to let
me out, he suggested perhaps we might make a climb later in the
week. I nodded.

But it was not to be that year. Two days later I was swept
away in a saturation slab avalanche, a mass of ice and snow
unleashed by its sheer water weight, and carried down four
hundred feet. I was buried chest deep in avalanche debris that
reached depths of twenty feet, and suffered a broken ankle and a
mangled knee. Tendons, ligaments, muscles had been torn. After
surgery, I recuperated for a week at Hamish's cottage before I
was well enough to return home. During this period of uncertainty about the recovery of my leg, the stay at Hamish's
cemented a friendship between us that cushioned the trauma of
the accident.

Hamish had a reputation that reached far beyond the narrow
realm of climbing. He was recognized worldwide as one of the
leading authorities on mountains and mountain rescue and had
been personally involved in hundreds of rescue missions. The
British government and the Queen herself had acknowledged
their debt of gratitude to him for his public service by awarding
him an O.B.E. But there was so much more to him. He was a
prolific writer—of rescue handbooks, novels, and nonfiction—

and a first-class adventurer. His travels had included, at the age
of twenty, a two-man assault on Mount Everest in the early 1950s
before it had ever been climbed. Subsequent trips had led him
from panning for gold in the jungles of New Guinea to searching
for lost tribes of blow-gun hunters in the Amazon basin, to
numerous hunts across the high Himalayas for the Abominable
Snowman. There was always an imminent expedition in
Hamish's future. And always a wealth of new ideas and concepts,
for Hamish's greatest forte was inventing. Whether he was
turning an old cast-off refrigerator into a dynamically balanced
wheelbarrow or creating the world's first all-metal ice ax (to
replace the weaker wood-metal combination), or designing a
portable hyperbaric oxygen decompression chamber, there was
no end to Hamish's fruitful creativity. While this diversity of
accomplishments thrust his name into public consciousness,
Hamish himself remained very much the retiring, low-profile
individual. So much so, there had grown about him a mysterious
mythlike aura. His commonplace activities were scrutinized with
undue curiosity. "But why does a single man like Hamish need
three hundred raspberry bushes—and all those fruit trees?"
Tongues were set a-wagging, whether strains of *Madama Butterfly*
were heard wafting from his cottage at all hours of the night as he
plotted out a new suspense thriller, or he was seen out collecting
bushels of elder flowers for another of his passions, winemaking.
With time the locals of the valley had come to dub him the elusive
"Fox of Glencoe." A title he did little to live down.

Later when I was back in America, the strength gradually
returned to my leg after intensive physiotherapy. During this
time of recovery, I designed a program of study about man in the
mountains and all their elements. I gathered curriculum outlines
from special mountain schools in Scotland, France, Germany,
and Switzerland. I combed the finer points of each and fashioned
my own plan. I called it orography, after the Greek word for
mountains, and submitted it to the University Without Walls, an
external degree program of the University of Massachusetts.

Initially they were less than ready to accept my proposal, but eventually they acknowledged my field of study.

Now the world became my classroom; the various experts of the mountain world, my teachers. That autumn Hamish wrote inviting me to come across and work with him. Dave and Ian would be there as well. In early winter I returned to the Highlands, and over the next years they became home. No matter where my education took me, be it to study the effects of the Alps on the people of Chamonix, or avalanche control in the Tetons to become a government certified snow ranger, I always returned to Scotland. Drinking in the Highland moors and rugged hills about me, I grew to love their untamed beauty. Before I knew it, I found myself changed, in a life of new rhythms and rituals. It was all I hoped a life could be: long arduous days on the hill, guiding, instructing, going on rescue missions, risking life and limb to save another's, making mountain films for BBC, ITV, *National Geographic*—creating art in so hostile an environment—or working with Hamish in his Mountain Rescue Laboratory assembling hand-made stretchers and testing out new theories, techniques, and equipment. Mind and body worked hard, their resources pushed to the limit time and again. They responded not by breaking down or even balking, but by growing strong, the body becoming sleek, resilient, hard, the mind honed to resolute, clear thinking, acute awareness. Hardly a day passed that I did not learn something I could use and carry with me, whether it was to read a slope for avalanche danger, to survive in a subarctic blizzard, or to comfort with compassion an accident victim's family. In my climbing too I grew, especially under the guidance of Hamish.

I remember one of those early days in Scotland—we were trying a new route on the Northeast Buttress of Ben Nevis. The way ahead was far from obvious amidst the overhanging rime-covered walls and great jumbled blocks of granite. I watched as Hamish moved upward with ease, not a movement wasted. He showed no apprehension about the line of the route. He did not try to force it in any one direction. It was as if the mountain spoke to him and he listened to its message. We climbed on. Before us gangways, ramps, chimneys, and seams appeared and disappeared below us as if by magic. In only three hours we sat basking in the sun on Ben Nevis' summit. From the lessons of that climb and the hundreds of climbs that were to follow over the next years, I gradually made the transition from proficient climber to well-rounded seasoned alpinist. To climb well was one thing, to climb safely in the mountains another thing entirely, requiring as much thought and knowledge as climbing techniques. Reading and interpreting conditions on a mountain, the snow, weather, temperature, oneself, recognizing subtle changes and being open to change at a moment's notice; making the right choice, be it retreating a mere fifty feet beneath the summit or pushing on in a raging blizzard: these were the hard-won skills developed only with time and experience. These were the things that kept one alive in the mountains, not climbing ability. Thus I passed from apprentice to alpinist.

For all Glencoe's remoteness in the western Highlands, one never felt the isolation at Hamish's cottage. A steady stream of visitors filtered through, from Everest mountaineers to Welsh rock climbers, from Nepalese Sherpas to African jungle explorers. There was no end of characters from the world over who sought Hamish out, and no end of communications that poured in daily. A letter from a scientist in the Antarctic on ice worms. A night cable from the People's Republic of China for more portable stretchers or an urgent call from Hollywood requesting safety advice for a motion picture. Merely being there brought a wealth of contacts and opportunities that would have been hard to match anywhere else. A memorable one was an invitation Hamish received in 1975 from the Mountaineering Federation of the USSR to attend a climbers' meet in the Bezinghi Region of the central Caucasus. His enthusiasm for visiting the area, which had been closed to outsiders for fifty years, was infectious; on the spot that dark and dreary February day in Glencoe he, Big Ian, and I found ourselves making plans for the trip in June. We would go as representatives of the Scottish Mountaineering Club. Things being what they are, plans don't always proceed as we would have them. A month before departure Hamish and Ian could not go, having more pressing commitments. With Hamish's encouragement that I shouldn't miss the opportunity of a lifetime, suddenly I found myself the sole SMC representative heading off to Russia.

At the Camp Bezinghi there were three hundred participants, the finest climbers from many Eastern Bloc nations: Czechs, Bulgarians, Estonians, Latvians, East Germans, Russians. Upon my arrival I found myself the only English-speaking person. Seeing my plight, the Russians kindly sent for Dr. Alexandro Kristoforich—"the professor," as I simply called him. An ancient and most venerable alpinist, he was one of the pioneers of Russian climbing and a professor of nuclear physics at Moscow University. He also had the ability to speak seven languages, including English, which saddled him with the unenviable task of being my translator, interpreter, and general companion. The early days of the meet were spent in acclimatizing ourselves to the new area and altitude, the professor and I blissfully strolling the meadows searching out exotic alpine wildflowers or collecting mushrooms and morels for the Russian-style picnics we lunched upon, spread on the tops of large boulders. Aged goat cheese, sour yak yogurt, black bread, fresh miniature fruits and vegetables—all prized specialities of the Georgian Caucasus—caviar, champagne, vodka by the liter: there was no scrimping. From the first it was obvious the Soviets aimed to please and impress, and they succeeded. This was less than true, unfortunately, when it came time for climbing. I soon discovered that mountaineering was a state-controlled activity in Russia, a branch of the government, and that the idea of hiking or climbing simply for enjoyment did not exist. There was no spirit of independence, so much a part of Western climbing, no feeling of limitless freedom when in the mountains. In the USSR, climbing was governed by a book of rules and regulations. Two of these particularly affected me as a lone foreign alpinist: solo climbing was forbidden, and only climbers of like nationalities could climb together.

After a week of prodding by the professor, the Federation in Moscow finally recognized my plight and allowed me an exemption. For the first time a team of Russian and American climbers would join together in a single rope, for an ascent of a five-thousand-meter peak. My ropemates were to be two Soviet Masters of Sport, Anatoli Markolof, young and lean, and the older, squat Annekt Peppin, one of Russia's leading mountain rescue experts. There was no discussion as to choice of routes for us. As always, the Federation decided such matters. We would attempt Djanghi-tau, North Face.

At 3 A.M., July 15, we roped up and set off across the glacier for our climb. I led the way, with Annekt in the middle and Anatoli bringing up the rear. We wove a path over the broken glacial surface, around gaping crevasses, across fragile snow bridges and hanging isthmuses of ice. Oftentimes, ground that I easily passed over gave way under the much heavier Annekt, who followed fifty feet behind. With a *whoosh* and a yell he would drop from view into the black hole that opened beneath his feet, swallowing him up. Immediately Anatoli and I braced ourselves for the inevitable shock of catching the two-hundred-pound load of Annekt on the rope tied between our waists. Each time Annekt fell, Anatoli and I were thrown to our knees, then dragged some yards toward the lip of the crevasse. Painfully, hand over hand, we hauled out Annekt, who was suspended between us on the taut rope. The security of the rope prevented a number of potential death falls down into the bowels of the glacier.

By first light we were on the lower slopes of the mountain, the three of us alternating the lead, sometimes climbing on rock, sometimes on ice, sometimes stretches of both. After the first several thousand feet it became apparent Djanghi-tau was not in perfect condition. A thin, treacherous mantle of snow masked the rock and ice over this part of the face. As the sun rose higher it melted this mask, but as we climbed, nearing the steeper, cleaner buttresses, ice avalanches of greater and greater proportion and frequency began rumbling and scouring down Djanghi-tau. Although they never posed any great threat to us, since our line followed a series of raised ridges on the face, the deafening roar and the sight of millions of tons of ice cascading down the mountain, first on the right, then on the left, then once more on the right, left us all a little unnerved. Eighteen-thousand-foot Djanghi-tau is a sharp, angular mountain, reminiscent of the Matterhorn, yet three thousand feet higher. The North Face is six thousand feet long and a fine climb, having a little bit of everything that makes a good mountain route—steep, solid, blood-red granite, narrow ice-choked gulleys, in places no more than a yard wide, broad hanging icefields shimmering in the sun like china platters, slender arêtes so delicate they matched the spines in a fish's back. The earlier delays in camp caused by red tape seemed very far away now. Only the twice-daily radio calls, morning and night, which we were required to make to base camp reminded us that Big Brother was still watching. Though neither Annekt nor Anatoli spoke any English nor I any Russian, our desire to work well together overcame the barrier. Gestures, expressions, and eyes did the work of words, unifying us into a strong, trusting team. On the morning of July 17, Annekt Peppin, Anatoli Markolof and I stood on the summit of Djanghi-tau. Within the hour the Apollo-Soyuz linkup took place overhead in space.

Those five weeks in southern Russia were all Hamish said they would be—the experience of a lifetime. Still it was Scotland and my life there that had developed in me the skills, expertise, knowledge and flexibility for the success I had in the Caucasus.

That fall when I returned to Scotland, Hamish, Ian, and I spent many an hour reliving the tales of our summer adventures. The close companionship of those days is the finest I have known, whether on the hill or simply supping on greasy fish and chips at Hell's Kitchen on those Thursday nights in Fort

William, afterward inhaling pints, wet and sweaty, shoulder to shoulder in the smoke-filled Jacobite Pub. In the end I found that the initially cold, hardened attitude of the Scots, at first so resistant and suspicious to the outsider, was much like an ice-skimmed pond. Once the surface had been cracked, the warmth and affection flowed forth from behind the brusqueness that is so much a part of the Scottish character.

The years I spent in Scotland went far beyond simple education, beyond the knowledge gained and talents developed and refined; the experience itself entered my soul, wrapping itself round me, shaping, forming, polishing the being I am today—projecting me in the direction I head today.

V

I am just a stranger
In this foreign land
An ocean of swirling faces
Darkened grains of sand

The soft nasal rasp of Harley's snoring catches my attention. I turn to look at him. It strikes me as funny that I can only conjecture what Harley's reasons are for going to Africa. We have never discussed even this. But here we sit on this jumbo jet traveling at over six hundred miles per hour together on our way to Africa, partners on our way to Kilimanjaro's Breach Wall. For all our differences, I feel Harley and I will make a good team. Our strengths, our incredible drive and determination coupled with Harley's rock-climbing ability and my detailed knowledge of mountains and years of ice-climbing and alpinism experience, complement each other, making for a very strong combination, effective and efficient. Certainly there have been stranger associations in history; for instance, the first two who conquered Everest. No two individuals could have been more disparate than Edmund Hillary, a New Zealand beekeeper, and his partner, Tenzing Norgay, a Nepalese Sherpa tribesman. Yet, some strange chemistry carried them to the highest point on earth. Likewise I expect the best from Harley and myself. I slouch back into my seat, before long engulfed by the deep relentless roar of the engines and by thoughts of Africa.

Africa. Like the massive stone head of some primitive cave

dweller's crude ax, it splits the waters of the Atlantic and Indian oceans with its immensity. In the north, the great Sahara Desert, larger in area than the United States, stretches from the Atlantic to the Red Sea. In the south, the burned sands of the Kalahari Desert and the salt flats of Etasha and Makarikari lie in the narrowing tooth of land that comes to a point in Cape Town. The center of the continent, lush jungles and grasslands nourished by plentiful tropical rainfall, is girded by the invisible belt of the equator. Though much of Africa rises over two thousand feet above sea level in the nature of a broad plateau, little of it is high mountainous terrain. Aside from the Atlas Range to the north-west in Morocco and Algeria, the principal heights are in East Africa, below the wrinkled highlands of Ethiopia. The countries of Kenya, Tanzania, and Uganda form a single raised land mass called the Great Lakes Plateau, in the midst of which, like a gem, shimmer the waters of Lake Victoria. The plateau is deeply furrowed by the Rift Valley, a geologic fault that runs the length of East Africa from the Red Sea to the Indian Ocean. During the course of history, the gradual fracturing along fault lines has created cracks, zones of weakness, allowing magma to rise to the earth's surface, forming gigantic volcanic cones, the highest peaks in Africa: Mount Kenya (Kenya), the Ruwenzori Range (Uganda) and Kilimanjaro (Tanzania). Only on these peaks, which lie virtually on the equator itself, can one find permanent African snow and glaciers. Tropical ice indeed! Like old, white-haired kings, the mountains reign over their encircling jungles and the broad plains that sweep off into the distance.

The squeal of tires on runway asphalt rouses Harley and me. It is early morning, December 30. The long journey—two in-flight movies and six meals long—is over. We peer out our porthole, anxious for a first view of the Dark Continent. There's little to see. The outside window glass is steamed over, dripping with condensation, something I have never seen happen to a jet window. Before long the plane lurches to a stop. Amidst the throng of sleepy American and British tourists, Harley and I shuffle toward the exit. Stepping from air-conditioned plane to rusting gangway adorned with the peeling blue lettering EAST AFRICAN AIRWAYS, I squint back the bright sunlight. Africa at last! But the first thing I notice is the heat. It is oppressive—not just hot. So humid. Especially for me: I am dressed for New England winter in heavy blue cord pants, wool turtleneck, fisherman sweater, and—beneath it all—a suit of mohair long underwear. In the final stages of packing, when push came to shove, I simply had no room for them, yet I hesitated to leave them behind. I could imagine one freezing night high in Africa's mountains when I would need the extra insulation. So I wore them. Now I would suffer for my pains. In the seconds it takes me to descend from top step of the gangway to runway I am moist with sweat. For relief, I hoist up sweater and shirt to remove them, then have second thoughts. Before me stands a single machine-gun-toting soldier. Nervously I flinch. A black man—with a gun. He is immaculately dressed in crisply pressed khaki shorts and shirtsleeves, complete with beret. He wears the insignia of sergeant. As I pass he greets me pleasantly, then directs me aside to wait with the remaining passengers. I'm really not sure if my uneasiness is caused by the man with the gun or by the black man with the gun. What would my reaction have been if he were an armed white soldier, like the Swiss military police at Geneva Airport? Here in Africa I suddenly realize that I am the minority—our roles are reversed.

When the lot of us have assembled, the sergeant escorts us toward the terminal. Harley and I walk the short hundred paces to the building in silence. Midway, a small metallic placard bids us: WELCOME TO KENYA. NAIROBI INTERNATIONAL AIRPORT. Even this limited exertion sprouts new rivers of perspiration from our foreheads. It runs down my neck and is absorbed by the wool collar of the turtleneck. In the bright sunlight Harley's hair glistens wet, as if he has just taken a swim.

Within, the terminal is breathless. No air-conditioning, no fan, no open windows, no movement of air at all. Just hot stale space filled with sweating, sticky bodies. There are more soldiers milling about, sporting snubby machine pistols and Uzi sub-machine guns. No one appears to give them any notice. All attention is focused on clearing immigrations and customs, to escape to the fresh air and freedom out-of-doors. As we stand in line, I examine my own misgivings about Africa, about coming. Have I made a mistake? Harley and I remain introspective, silent. Within our silence there is a certain agreed dejection between us, as if to say, "Who knew it was going to be like this? Did we blow it!"

Our turn comes eventually. We shoulder our gear and head out the heavy grate doors. A sultry breeze blows across our faces and matted hair. At last, freedom! What a contrast to the world of winter at home. The airport is located ten miles east of Nairobi on a great open grassy plain. Date palms, coconut palms, banana trees. It is green, lush, and beautiful. Flowers are blooming everywhere. Harley and I crack smiles at each other simul-taneously. Misgivings melt away, forgotten. We scan the throng of people languishing in the shade beneath the terminal's tin awning. A sea of black faces, dotted with an occasional lighter visage. Most of the latter belong to tourists or to the Sheraton and Hilton employees come to collect them for the hotels. They certainly dress for the part, sporting classic khaki safari outfits and leopard-skin-banded bush hats cocked slightly off center, John Wayne style. Iain Allen, our Kenyan contact, is nowhere to be seen. Will I still recognize him, or he me? It has been six years since we met in Scotland—and only that once, down in Duror. Dave introduced us that alcohol-laced evening. The lads had come down from the Fort and the Glen. We had a real all-night session. To be truthful, I have only the haziest recollection now as to what Iain really looks like. Tall, thin; brown hair, I think. Not much more. Harley and I keep watch, waiting for the crowd to thin out. When all white faces have departed and still no Iain, we decide to phone him.

Although the phone box looks like the conventional English

model, the English dialing instructions have been obilterated, leaving only the Swahili, which neither of us can read. Harley tries first, dialing out the number Iain has given us, and promptly loses several shillings. Again he tries. No luck. Then again. In minutes he is changeless, reduced to fisticuffs with the bandit phone box. I rush off to the bank for more change. Then it's my turn to be frustrated. I dial out 484-23. It's a simple number, really—hard to imagine anything difficult about it. At the sound of the *bip-bip-bip* I drop in the coins and wait. As in a Las Vegas slot machine, the money clinks as it drops within the bowels of the phone box. There is a slight pause, then my call is disconnected and reverts back to the buzz of an open line. Again and again I repeat the procedure. No luck. After my thirteenth attempt I give up. Somehow I feel I'd have better odds in Las Vegas. Several Kenyan pounds lighter, we decide to forgo the call and take a taxi to Iain's house in town.

We gather our packs and kit bags and haul them the short distance toward the nearest waiting cab, a battered black Renault. The driver slouches on the right front fender, head low to one side, seemingly asleep. Yet as soon as we make a move toward him he springs to life, bounding from his perch to give us a hand. He dumps half our load unceremoniously into the car's trunk, heaving the remainder up on the roof rack, a roof rack with no bottom supports. The hollow reverberating sound of buckling metal fills the air as the roof dimples, then caves in six inches under the weight. Our driver takes it all in stride, jumping up on the front seat and pushing the sagging bubble of metal up with his back. Nimbly he drops down to the driver's seat, saying, "Hok-ay! Wha-ra-yu gunna-ton?"

For a few seconds we stare at him dumbly. Obviously we know from the rising tone of his voice he has asked us a question, but what was it?

I recover first, saying, "We want to go into town. To Nairobi."

He says, "Yaas, Ny-RO-bi," smiling and shaking his head in affirmation. Then he adds, "Whar-der?"

"Ah . . . Ah . . .," I stammer. "We want to go to 67 Covent Crescent."

"Hunh?" It is easy to see from his squint and the wrinkling of his brow that he does not understand.

I repeat, speaking slowly, "The . . . address . . . is . . . 6-7 . . Covent . . . Crescent."

He only wags his head. I slump against an awning support.

Harley takes over to give it a try. He speaks forcibly, loudly, enunciating every syllable, "WE WANT TO GO NEAR NAIROBI!"

Instantly our driver brightens, "Yaas. Ny-RO-bi!"

Harley continues, "THE PLACE IS 67 COVENT CRES-CENT."

Just as quickly the light goes out of his face. He frowns. "Da-nowa." Again he is shaking his head.

Undaunted, Harley slips a thick rectangular notebook out of his sack and opens it to a blank page. With a thick felt-tipped marker he fills the page with a bold "67" followed below by "COVENT CRESCENT." He smiles as he hands it across to the driver. "Watch, this will do it, Rob."

The cabby takes hold of the tablet, studying it carefully for some seconds, then promptly turns it upside down and studies it some more. Harley's grin vanishes. Our driver hands back the tablet, once more shaking his head in bewilderment.

Ideas exhausted, we are just about to reconcile ourselves to a long walk when help arrives in the form of a young passing Kenyan. He stops and asks us in perfect flowing English, decidedly Sandhurst-tinged, "May I be of some service to you gentlemen?" Gladly we hand our burden over to him. A minute's rapid-fire discourse in Swahili replete with wild gestures and we're on our way.

In twenty minutes we arrive at Iain's. Three yard boys quickly abandon their work on the colorful beds of flowers to greet us at the wrought-iron gate. It's hard to believe we are in Africa. The stone country house and its quiet English garden look as if they have been transported from the Lake District of England.

Iain is a sometime artist, sometime art dealer, presently full-time operator of Tropical Ice, a guide service covering all of East Africa. As soon as I set eyes on him, all my haziness about him fades away. He is just as he was in Scotland—animated in a relaxed sort of way. Perhaps the hair is a bit longer, but he is much the same, tall, deeply tanned, and thin. He is in fact more strikingly slender than I remember. In Africa only a few hours, I am already aware of the drastic differences in body stature that exist between East Africa and Britain or America. Black or white, rich or poor, everyone here is much thinner, less bulky, almost devoid of the body fat of their more northerly counterparts. Could it be the extreme heat in this equatorial part of the world that's responsible? When I ask Iain, he just laughs.

As luck would have it, we have arrived at a most opportune time. Tomorrow Iain and his climbing partner, Ian Howell, will be going up to Mount Kenya. They welcome Harley and me to join them, as long as we are not too fatigued from our journey. We jump at the opportunity, eager to escape to the hills again. Likewise, the sooner we begin acclimatization and learning about these strange equatorial mountains, the better prepared we will be for Kili and the Breach Wall. Climbing communities in Africa are small tightly knit groups few and far between, made up mostly of colonials who picked up the sport on their home hills. Here again we're lucky. No two climbers in East Africa presently know more about its mountains, the peculiarities of conditions, weather and seasons, than do the two Ians, who have the experience of hundreds of climbs over many years. Better than anyone else, they know the current status of all the climbs in these mountains, which ones are improving, which deteriorating. Just this past week before our arrival both of them were up on Mount Kenya. A month earlier Iain Allen had been into the area on Kili leading to the Breach Wall that Harley and I hope to explore. There is much the two Ians could show us about East Africa and East African climbing.

We are up before dawn the next morning packing gear into Iain's white wagon. The night has brought no coolness. It is still stifling hot. Before the car is half loaded, we have stripped to tees and running shorts, sopping with sweat. Under the weak yellow cast of the car's interior dome light Iain informs me, "It's hard to imagine that where we're going, only one hundred miles from here, it's probably below zero degrees right now." I agree: that is fairly unfathomable.

A shadow glides silently toward us out of the darkness. It is Ian Howell. He leans into the sparse light. "Morning, Iain—lads." He slings the pack from his shoulder into the rear of the car. We pile in and are off for the mountain.

After thirty minutes' journey the dawn breaks. Harley and I have our first views of African countryside. We are on a great flat plain. The amber stubble of dry grass, dotted green with the occasional shrub or bush, spreads unbroken as far as eye can see. The highway slashes uniformly like a great gray pencil line, straight as if drawn with a ruler. Several times the Ians point out herds of animals—giraffe, zebra, wildebeest. But they are miles off, indistinguishable to all but trained eyes. From the moving vehicle Harley zeroes in with his 500-millimeter lens on several herds for a closer view, but still they appear as little more than fleas inspected at arm's length. The immensity of the land is staggering, as is the changeability.

Without warning we cross some ill-defined line and are among lush green knolls and hills. The road curves and switches back, hugging the rumpled lay of the land. Scattered banana shambas and coffee plantations suddenly appear, dotting the roadside. We pass several small villages, but their thatch-roofed houses appear deserted. Not a person stirs. Still, above and behind, the hillsides are draped with someone's handiwork. Acre upon acre of batik fabric lies over the knolls, stretched from post to post to dry. In the morning sunshine their brilliant colors glow, blues, reds, yellows, greens. It is a work of art paying homage to the natural environment all around. Harley and I are full of questions.

Where are all the people? What are these villages doing in the middle of nowhere? How do the people survive? Why the drastic change in the countryside? Especially in the vegetation? The two Ians look to each other with amusement.

"You'll find East Africa little like most places you've been before. It takes some getting used to," Ian Howell explains. "In areas like this you have to be careful not to be fooled by your eyes. Don't confuse what you see with what is really there."

Despite its appearance as only untamed bush and surrounding jungle—wilderness uninhabited save for a few clusters of people scratching out a meager roadside existence—this area is one of the most prosperous and populated in all Kenya. The vegetation is a thick curtain which hides much. Half a million people live here, most working small farms of coffee and bananas, many making handcrafts such as woven baskets, others working in light industries similar to the dye-batik plant we passed earlier. "The batik plant," they call it! An ill-conceived name for such a place, for nothing here fits my image of the word "plant." There are no great rows of grimy warehouses, no belching stacks filled with sooty smoke, no tanks strung with miles of convoluted pipeline, no crashing sound of mighty pistons. Nothing could be less appropriately named. Then again, perhaps in another way "plant" describes this place perfectly. Like a plant it rises out of the surrounding vegetation, at one with it, as if spawned by it.

Iain tells us that we have left the plain that makes up most of East Africa and entered the foothills that lie beneath Mount Kenya. Though the mountain may still be far away, hidden from view, he explains, this area is an extension of it and very much under its influence.

The weather, for example. Clouds over the plains we crossed this morning heat up from the sun. Wind currents carry them along to this area we're going through now, much higher than the plain, thus pushing the clouds higher up into the atmosphere. At this greater height in the sky the air temperature is cooler. Water vapor in the clouds cools, condenses and falls as rain, plentiful rain, which supports the rich vegetation we see. Throughout the world I have seen great mountains exert a certain control upon terrain surrounding them, but nowhere is the effect more profound or sudden.

We ride on in silence for a while, watching the scenery blur by. Then, as usually is the case with climbers, the topic of climbing crops up: the different areas we've been to, the climbs we've done. Harley and then Ian Howell talk of the sea cliffs of Anglesey, which gird the coast of north Wales. In the form of Holyhead Mountain, looking out toward Ireland, the rose-colored granite drops smoothly and vertically into the heaving Irish Sea. Harley recently finished a television film there for ABC-TV. He did some great routes, even pulling off the first solo ascent of the Strand, a long, sinister slit on the face of the sea cliff, varying from an inch to six inches wide, covered by greasy algae and droppings from the sea birds which nest in it. In their own muted way the two Ians appear impressed. In the climbing world the Strand is known as an extreme climb, continually sustained, with almost no places to stop and rest. To solo it without a rope or safeguards is to climb a "death route"—one slip, one small mistake, and you are a goner. Ian Howell knows it well, being originally from England and at the forefront of British climbing before he moved to Kenya a dozen years ago. Still, he doesn't regret being out of the mainstream. He says he rarely, if ever, misses the crowded, rushed life of the United Kingdom. In Africa he has gone his own way, charting out new areas in his life, work and climbing. Ian does not need the outside impetus of competition with others to excel. He sets his own lofty goals and standards. He certainly looks as if life here agrees with him. Tall, lean, deeply suntanned, he looks more like twenty-five than the forty years he is. Only when he breaks into raucous laughter does one have a hint of his age, from the tiny crow's feet radiating out from joyous blue eyes.

Iain Allen brings up Yosemite in California, which, aside from Mount Kenya and Kili, is his favorite place on earth to climb.

The narrow glacially gouged valley is a rock climber's paradise, its sides lined with polished granite walls. Warm, sunny day after day, the rock is the finest and the most beautiful he has ever seen. And there are miles of it—more than one could climb in a lifetime. This past year, on a visit there, he climbed the Nose of El Capitan, a three-thousand-foot prow of rock that thrusts upward at the entrance of Yosemite Valley like the bow of some giant battleship. This spring he plans to return to do the difficult Sentinel West Face, which stands guard over Yosemite Valley like a great stone watchtower, several thousand feet of vertical granite. It usually takes two to three days to do this route. Iain, wondering aloud, as much to himself as to Harley, says he doesn't see how anyone could possibly do *that* climb in two and a half hours. It seems beyond the capabilities of any man. We all know it isn't, though. Several years earlier, on one of his infrequent trips to Yosemite, Harley went up one morning and free-soloed The Sentinel in that incredibly short time. No partner, no rope, no safeguards. The feat stunned the climbing world. For a few, mainly jealous competitors in rock climbing, it was a case of sour grapes. They said here were the doings of a maniacal egotist, half crazed by vanity and the lust for limelight. But the majority of climbers were in awe of his achievement. He had done something that seemed humanly impossible. Among his peers in the United States, it was predicted that with time this climb would be looked upon as one of the most important in the history of American climbing—on par with the climbs of Cassin and Bonatti in the Alps. Likewise many felt certain his presence would influence the direction and flow of U.S. climbing in the eighties and nineties as profoundly as those two premiere alpinists changed that of the Alps in the thirties, forties and fifties.

At this time Harley already has a reputation that precedes him worldwide. Wherever he goes he has become accustomed to the throngs of adoring, back-slapping fans. Sycophants buy him drinks and pay for his meals, all just for his presence, just for a few words of conversation with him. Africa has been different. From the first, the two Ians have appeared remarkably subdued, happy to see us and all, but seemingly unaware of or unimpressed by his reputation. Harley noticed it straightaway. It bothered him, or so he told me. Now, as we continue to talk climbing, I sense a change in them, slight but discernible. They are relaxing, more friendly, warmer. And, yes, I am certain, they *are* impressed by Harley and by the things he has accomplished.

Soon we pass the small village of Naro Moro. Iain brakes and gestures up and rightward out his window. "There she is, lads! Only twenty miles now." Through the bluish mist of morning, the horizon is dominated by a dark form, a great uplifted pyramid. Backlit by the rising sun, in deep shadow, the subtleties of Mount Kenya are lost to the eye, but the profile she presents is awesome.

Unlike any other mountain I have seen, Mount Kenya rises not amidst a range of peaks or chain of mountains, but vaults skyward in regal isolation. Harley and I stare entranced. Iain speeds up again, and in seconds Mount Kenya recedes once more behind a wall of vegetation.

"Well, what do you think?" Ian Howell breaks the silence.

"That's something!" I reply.

"Sure is!" adds Harley.

Iain Allen laughs, "If you think Mount Kenya's impressive, wait till you see Kilimanjaro. Kenya's a wart next to Kili." The comparison went right by Harley and me. For the moment Mount Kenya was big enough, and the only thing on our minds. "Now that you've seen her, have you any notions of particular climbs you'd like to do?" asks Iain. "That side we looked straight onto back there in the clearing, the West Face, is always in perfect shape this time of year."

"What about the Diamond Ice Couloir?" I ask. "We're really looking for a training climb here in Kenya very similar to Kili's Breach Wall. The Diamond Ice Couloir seems the perfect choice, doesn't it?"

"Yes, but the Couloir is really a winter climb. That is, winter as defined here in the Southern Hemisphere—July, August, even September, October." Iain explains that Mount Kenya and, to a lesser degree, Kilimanjaro straddle the Equatorial Zone. The sun rises and sets over them in an almost perfect east-west line. In the course of a year, the subtle shift in the earth's position relative to the sun creates an exaggerated seasonal change, a change that makes for opposite seasons on opposing sides of the mountain at the same time. Here now in January the southern flanks of Mount Kenya, the half containing the Diamond Ice Couloir, bask in the warm sunshine of summer. Flowers bloom, grass and plants are alive and thriving. It is a time to do rock climbs now, staying clear of rotting ice routes and avalanche-prone gullies. Iain patiently advises us that if we want ice climbing we must circle round to the northern flanks of the mountain, which now stand clenched in the grip of winter, whipped by icy gales, plastered with powder snow and deep-blue bulges of ice.

Harley asks, "So, is the Diamond unclimbable now, or is it just not in the best condition?"

Ian answers, "Of course, it is probably climbable. The first ascent was achieved at this very time several years ago. But this year there is much more snow. It might make for a very dangerous undertaking requiring perfect timing, extreme speed, utmost care and, perhaps most of all, luck. In the end, who can say? Conditions here in East Africa are extremely variable from one day to the next. There are rarely severe sustained storms, but there is continual weather change. One morning things are perfect, by afternoon it's raining, even up to sixteen thousand feet. You'll soon see that one must bide his time. You can't try to rush or force anything."

To prove his point he tells us of the grisly fate that befell six RAF climbers back in the early sixties. It was just this time of year, January. They were crossing beneath the Diamond Couloir when it avalanched. There was nowhere to run, nowhere to hide. All six were killed instantly, crushed under a thousand tons of snow moving at a hundred miles an hour. There had been many other accidents as well, most of them occurring this very time of year. Not in the winter season of August or September.

Harley sits pensive for a time, then asks, "What about Kili? Isn't the Breach Wall the same exposure as the Diamond Couloir? Won't it have exactly the same bad conditions?"

Both Ians agree there is a chance that we might experience some warmth or melting. But Kilimanjaro and particularly the Breach Wall are much higher than Mount Kenya—almost 2,500 feet higher. The added altitude pushes it into the polar air which surrounds the jet stream this time of year. On their many trips into Kilimanjaro, both Ians recount, the major obstacle they faced was the cold. This is heartening news, for we have come well prepared for the coldest of temperatures.

The two Ians inquire now what other plans besides the Diamond Ice Couloir we may have on Mount Kenya. To be truthful, we have left it pretty much open. It is to be a time of training, for fitness and altitude, in preparation for Kili.

Harley answers, and I began to realize that he has more on his mind than he has expressed. "Unfortunately I've got a very tight time schedule on this trip to Africa. Rob can stay on, but I've got to get back to be in Houston the morning of January twenty-third. Anyway, I'd like to take maximum advantage while I am here and do four or five routes on Mount Kenya over the next week." Both Ians' eyes pop wide open in amazement. Harley continues, "If possible, tomorrow I'd like to get the Couloir out of the way. It might not be so good, but it'll make great lecture material, for it's what everybody in America wants to hear about. The next day I'd like to free-climb the Diamond Buttress route, and the next perhaps free Bailey's route on Point John. The following day maybe we can all do a new route together."

The two Ians grin and break into laughter.

"He's having us on, isn't he?" says Iain, nudging me with his elbow. "It's a joke. Right?" One look at Harley's deadpan expression, however, and the giddiness vanishes.

"You can't be serious, Harley?" says Ian Howell. Harley's glare says that he is.

A sobered Iain Allen fervently continues, "I don't think you understand, Harley. Mount Kenya rises to over seventeen thousand feet. That's two thousand feet higher than any point in Europe. This is not like climbing in the Alps. The routes on Mount Kenya *begin* one thousand feet higher than the summit of Mount Blanc. It's a whole different ball game here."

Harley smirks.

Ian Howell tries a different tack. "The features that attract most people to Mount Kenya, its sheer verticality, the way it juts straight up, and the mountain's easy accessibility—these are exactly the reasons that make it such a dangerous mountain. Countless numbers have died on the slopes of Mount Kenya from high-altitude sickness. It is so easy to go too high too fast. Then it is usually too late. There are no rescue teams waiting here on call like in America. Nor are there any helicopters standing by to pluck you off the mountainside like in Yosemite. Mount Kenya is too high for them—above their flying ceiling." I do not know the impression the two Ians have made on Harley, but their advice seems sound to me.

"Ian and I have a lot of experience on these mountains," says Iain Allen. "Over the years it's been rare when we can manage more than two good routes a week on Mount Kenya. Very occasionally we have pushed more in a single week, but then only by pressing total exhaustion and taking a fortnight for recovery afterward."

Harley, silent all this while, appears to have absorbed the point the two have been making. He speaks now. "All of what you say is interesting and well taken. You speak for yourselves in your experience in East Africa, which I'm sure is great. Certainly much greater than mine or Rob's. Still, different people can view the same thing very differently. One person tries a climb and cannot do it. Another solos it the first time. The first says, 'It's impossible!' The second says, 'It's a piece of cake!' Who's right? In my travels this has happened time and time again. In Australia, Norway, East Germany. By the time I return home, the record is usually set straight."

Harley has made his point. He says no more. We ride on in silence, the asphalt now having given way to a dusty gravel roadbed, the short access road leading to the Mount Kenya National Park. I slouch in my seat trying to soften the bumps and turn over in my mind what has been said this morning. I realize I would do well to keep the two Ians' advice in mind. What they were saying blended in with my own experience and reading. Yet all that Harley said is also true. He has proved it—time after time—exploding myth-inflated balloon after balloon. He made a career out of doing it. Can both notions be opposed to each other, yet still be true? Perhaps it depends upon the individual. After another fifteen minutes of jouncing on steadily deteriorating track, we reach the end of the line. Iain backs uphill onto a patch of angled turf. He says it'll give him a running start on the way home, just in case. We heave out the clutter of gear from the rear of the wagon and divvy it up. In fifteen minutes we're under way, following a well-worn path. In the humid heat, bent under our forty-pound loads, we sweat heavily. Each of us puffs breathlessly, unused to the exertion, even the two Ians despite their conditioning. As superb a creature of adaptation as man is, I conclude that the combination of 100-degree temperatures and strenuous labor is beyond his adaptive capability.

There is no spare energy for talk. Soon enough, the two Ians, Harley, and I find our own comfortable walking paces. We drift apart, each in his own little realm of sweat and toil. For me it is a time to think. A time for fantasy to catch up with reality. Yes, I am really in Africa, the Dark Continent. I am even hiking up the lower reaches of Mount Kenya. The dense vegetation of the rain forest gives way now to open woods almost like a scrubby poplar forest in the White Mountains of New Hampshire, yet the silver trees and yellow shrubs are like no species I know. It's true! The next two weeks will be the most exciting, interesting of my life. I am certain. There's so much to see, so much to do. All of it new, like stepping into another world.

Higher up I break out onto an open heather heath just like Scotland, and just as boggy. I sink knee deep into the viscous black peat with each step. So absorbed am I in my thoughts, my eyes locked groundward guiding my every step, I only now notice the change in weather. It has clouded over and now begins to rain. I pull on my anorak, hoist on my sack, and once more plod ahead, leaving my hood down. The rain is welcome relief from the heat. I imagine the water droplets sizzling to steam on my forehead, as though flung against a hot wood stove. Hour upon hour I slog on. The rain steadily worsens. I lose all track of time and of the two Ians and Harley. Heavy shrouds of mist blanket the landscape, blotting out all features. Africa? I could as easily be in Scotland, Maine, or Mexico for all I can see. Out of the fog occasional groups pass me by, valley bound. Germans, Italians, Japanese—like faceless meandering mannequins in their bright colors, they flee the ramparts of Mount Kenya for some sanctuary far below.

In the half-light of dusk I fetch up at a flat-topped boulder resembling a stone bench. It has stopped raining, but a slate-gray overcast remains. I drop down onto the rock, aching, tired, and cold. The temperature has dropped steadily all day as I have climbed. Now I am chilled. I slip off my pack and change into dry woolen trousers and a sweater. What an improvement! Immediately I feel warmer. I drink from a small nearby stream clouded with the new rain runoff. It gushes downhill, swollen beyond its moss-lined banks. The water is icy, so cold it gives a momentary headache.

I gaze into the churning flow. Three years earlier, this very time of year, my friend Yvon Chouinard was here on Mount Kenya. He made the first ascent of the Diamond Ice Couloir on that trip. Later, in his usual understated way, he would tell me, "The Couloir is a beautiful line, a great climb but not *so* difficult.

There's really only one tough bit to deal with, the headwall, and of course the altitude." It didn't seem to matter to him that in the subsequent two years the couloir came to be classified as the most difficult ice climb in Africa and one of the most difficult in the world.

Understatement was typical of Yvon, in his climbing and in his life. In the late fifties, while working as an itinerant blacksmith, he had come to realize that most climbing equipment in America was imported from Europe. He knew he could make climbing hardware as good as if not better than the Europeans—and cheaper. The Chouinard Equipment Company was born, Yvon its sole employee. Today, twenty years later, his vision and sense of aesthetics in design and development have made Chouinard equipment for alpinists the most respected and sought-after mountaineering gear throughout the climbing world. The larger-than-life reputation that has grown up around his name often-times leaves Yvon a bit red faced. Upon meeting him, people cannot accept this five-foot-five-inch boyish-looking figure as Yvon Chouinard, America's "Prophet of Purism."

Yvon jokes that they always expect a hoary old man with shoulder-length white hair and a great flowing beard. Somehow in all this, instead of becoming the epitome of the harried, fast-aging executive complete with three-piece suit, Yvon remains himself, with faded blue jeans, tousled windblown hair and wool shirt. Instead of the company controlling his life, shackling him to a desk, he utilizes it as a means of financial security, freeing himself for some of the things he treasures in life—mountains, climbing, surfing, exploring.

In our climbing together Yvon and I traveled half the world, doing routes in the Alps, the Rockies, the Sierras, Scotland, and the limestone cliffs of southern France. Each of us was deadly serious about his climbing and his commitment to it. Still, what made our relationship click was that neither of us took ourselves too seriously. Stormed off a route in Chamonix, we were quite happy to go herb picking or truffle hunting in Provence or across to Courmayeur for a big pasta feed. Rained off Mount Robson in the Canadian Rockies, we were more than content to pass the days idly fly-fishing on the Old Man River in Alberta. Ours was a friendship without competition and without necessity, even the necessity of having to do a particular climb. We had nothing to prove to each other—other than our enjoyment of doing things together, be it climbing or otherwise. I sorely miss Yvon on this trip now. Somehow already it has taken on an air of severity that is alien to my love of mountains and climbing.

I look up, wondering, Where are the two Ians and Harley? Could they have passed me in the mist and already be in camp? I imagine a warm cozy hut, a hot brew awaiting my arrival, and dinner simmering on the stove. The image is encouraging. Far below I see two specks, themselves separated by a fair distance. I search for a third behind them, but see none. It can't be they— there are only two. Within ten minutes the front figure surges up the knob before me. It is Iain Allen. He tells me Ian and Harley are behind, coming soon. I'm surprised he looks so well—no worse for wear from the day's long journey. He says that after a hundred or so times one develops a certain fitness for the hike, which unfortunately is not matched by a growth of enthusiasm for it. For him the walk is pure drudgery. We sit waiting for the others.

Ian Howell soon arrives. He is a bit winded but still smiling, going strong as a horse. Ten minutes later Harley comes into view, as dour and huffy as the storm clouds above, and like them rumbling angrily. He curses, yet no one says a word for fear of releasing what little is restrained. We rest in silence the next few minutes, then prepare for the final half hour's journey to the hut. Fortunately it's level all the way, Ian tells us, even downhill in a few places.

We have just set off when black skies above part as if by magic. Where only seconds before loomed boiling clouds, now stands the immense southern wall of Mount Kenya. It rears up golden in the shaft of dying amber sunlight. Up, up, up to the twin pointed summits of Nelion and Batian. The two Ians, Harley, and I gaze motionless at the scene. The face is completely devoid of snow or ice save for a slender thread of white which falls vertically between the two peaks, slashing the mountain in half. This glistening gem is the Diamond Ice Couloir. It casts an aura of delicate fragility in the narrow perfection of its line, yet it simultaneously images a bold and brazen directness in its skyward sweep. Simply it is one of the most beautiful lines I have seen—anywhere in the world. Ian Howell produces a pair of mini-binoculars. We all have a quick look at the mountain. Then the two Ians study the face.

"Incredible! It has rained all the way up to seventeen thousand feet. See the rime line just below the summit? Tomorrow will be a perfect day. It's a go for the buttress. It looks great."

"And the Diamond Couloir?"

Iain Allen scans the line up and down with the glasses. On edge, Harley and I await the verdict. Finally it comes.

"It's OK." Iain continues to look. "Actually, it's better than OK; it appears almost perfect." Still, to be completely safe, he warns us to beat the warm summer sun, which at this time of year could turn the whole Couloir from frozen security to deadly slush in only a matter of hours. "Begin before first light tomorrow, move quickly and you should be all right."

It is amazing what a change of weather can do for the spirit. Harley's attitude has made a 180-degree turnabout. He is exuberant, full of animated chatter.

Under magenta twilight, buoyantly we glide the last miles to the hut. To food. To sleep. To tomorrow.

Under cover of darkness, Harley and I are off for the Couloir. It is a frosty morn. Nose hairs prickle from the bitter air. Blindly we wander upward, in search of our elusive line. There is only the starshine to go by. We skirt around jumbled mounds of talis piled high like great tottering building blocks. The sun is but a tinge of rouge to the east when we reach the bottom edge of the ice. Even in the half-light of predawn the icefield dazzles white. Hurriedly Harley and I strap on our gear. We are locked in a race against the sun. To save time we set off soloing the lower ice-field. Conditions are perfect. Ice axes and crampon points sink into the 45-degree ice as if it were Styrofoam, yet its surface glistens like glass. We bound up the slope at a near run—two hundred feet, three hundred, four hundred.

We are at the start of the Couloir and the first major difficulty, a slender dagger's blade of ice one hundred feet high. It is dead vertical and in places little more than a transparent veneer of ice, so thin you can see the ryolite rock crystals of the mountain behind. We tie onto the rope, and Harley takes the lead. I remain below to belay and safeguard him. He moves up the pitch smooth and steady, effortlessly handling every obstacle. It is a joy to watch him move. Yesterday's long approach hike is not for Harley, but this certainly is. He tops the wall. I hasten to follow after him. The sun's amber light eats away at the mountain's deep-blue shadow beneath us. We race on and up, rope length after rope length, exchanging leads in perfect teamwork. The valley shrinks far below as we gain height. It is a great day to be alive, to be in the mountains, to be here with Harley, moving together in a masterful synchronization in tune with the won-drous elements of rock, ice, and air. Mount Kenya is not an adversary to fear, to beat into submission, but a friend, a companion to Harley and me. Before we know it, we have passed the three-quarter mark of the Couloir, and arrive beneath the final obstacle.

A broad barrier of ice bars the way before us. It rises some 250 feet straight up to great curtains of icicles themselves thirty to forty feet long. Should the sun melt their precious glue, I can well imagine the consequences. They would rip through a body like a razor-honed saber. I hurry on. It is my lead, and the sunlight is but yards beneath us now. Time is of the essence. I tackle the headwall straight on, taking the most direct line up. It goes quickly but is very strenuous. Left arm and leg anchored on the crest of a bulging prow of ice, I bridge across with the right side of my body to the remainder of the wall to ease the angle. I arrive at the top exhausted, sucking for air, awash in a sea of sweat—but still ahead of the sun. From the nose of the prow I tiptoe leftward only yards beneath the icicles for a few tense moments, and I am out from beneath them, safe around a rock corner. Immediately Harley follows. He dashes up the wall in a blaze of speed. Yet for each step he moves up the wall, the sun matches his advance. It is neck and neck all the way. Harley anchors his two axes at my feet and hauls up on them to stand beside me. He is flushed, red as a beet and gasping. The day's first rays of sunlight stream from behind Point John and run across my face. Still recovering his breath, Harley hoarsely whispers to me, "Great lead! I don't know how you did it."

The compliment catches me by surprise, for Harley gives them rarely. As the sun sweeps upward toward the summit, morning's shadow is banished. It matters little now. The Couloir is finished. We have only the easy four-hundred-foot snowfield to reach the summit. In the full light of day now we don our dark glacier glasses to protect against the brilliant reflection off ice and snow that can quickly cause snow blindness and permanent eye damage at this altitude. We move left to a rock ledge for a badly needed rest and breakfast, sitting with legs dangling over the edge. It is like a very high open-air balcony. All of Africa lies at our feet. Gazing out, I feel the freedom of that small boy on Osceola—like a bird soaring free through the sky.

Too soon it is time for us to leave our airy perch. Stiffly we stir to finish our upward journey. Before long we make a stark discovery. With each step we sink up to our crotches in soft sticky snow. It is like oatmeal. Then, time and again, we must dig free the entombed limb and repeat the process. It is slow and tiring, a fight for every inch up the slope. At this rate the small four-hundred-foot snowfield will take us longer to pass than the whole of the Couloir beneath us. More importantly, though, it is dangerous. Mortally so, for surrounding us a hundred thousand tons of sodden snow sit in delicate balance. Constantly pulled upon by gravity, a chunk of ice, a fist-sized snowball, anything could trigger the whole mass into motion downhill. Down it would spill, leaping over the headwall into the lower Couloir. Down two thousand feet, carrying us along.

Treading as lightly as possible, we move leftward, aiming for the safety of the rock wall that borders the snowfield. The wall itself appears impenetrable, but its cracks and fissures offer secure anchors. Hands on rock, feet on snow, we follow its jagged curving edge, making a long circuitous route toward the summit. Our detour is twice the length of the normal route that goes straight up the snowfield's center to the top. What is little more than an easy twenty minutes' walk under normal conditions today becomes a six-hour trek. The sun beats down mercilessly, burning us like an oven's broiler. We crawl along. The endless work, coupled with dehydration, takes its toll. Patience wears thin. Harley's mood grows angry. Wildly he thrashes forward, leaving a deep trough behind him. He slashes his ice ax into the slush around him as if he meant to do the mountainside mortal harm, issuing forth a steady stream of oaths and curses, culminating in his refusal, after four exchanges of lead, to share the burden of our pack. I take it on myself. It shouldn't be, but for some reason I find it all strangely amusing.

Harley is relatively new to climbing mountains and has little tolerance yet for this slush-slogging or the long wet approach marches of yesterday. Not that anyone finds them enjoyable, but they are unavoidable integral parts of alpinism, as much as the glorious sunrises, the glistening water ice and firm red granite. How different his attitude would be now if the soggy slope before us were instead a sheer wall of sandstone or an overhanging ice wall. But it isn't.

Several times, after having negotiated especially nasty leads of bottomless porridge, Harley insists we abandon our ridiculous route and head for the center line. Each time I stand my ground, holding out for our present course. He stares at me, eyes afire, but says nothing. I sense that his mood results more from his overwhelming frustration than from actually wanting to change the route. After all, even for seasoned alpinists this has got to be one of the most trying of mountain situations, for it requires none of your many technical skills, just strength, effort and wells of patience. Harley the rock glider, while short on the last quality, bites the bullet and marshals impressive amounts of strength and effort as we dig and slog on.

Shadows grow long and stringlike in the waning hours of afternoon. At last only one hundred feet remain of the snowfield. It is Harley's lead. He strikes off in a beeline for the top, abandoning the rock wall. Up, up he heaves himself, crabbing rightward and moving ever closer to a ragged screen of melting icicles. I watch horrorstruck as he begins to pass directly beneath them, apparently oblivious to the danger they pose. When after a few minutes he still does not alter his course, I shout to him, "Look above you! Get back to the left!" He stops, glancing round and analyzing the situation for some seconds, then heeds my advice. Nonchalantly he wanders back leftward out of death's way. It is a small, uneventful incident, yet it troubles me. It could well have spelled tragedy for both of us.

I plod up, hugging the wall, to join him at the Gate of the Mists, the small col marking the end of the technical climbing. As I pull over the final hummock of snow topping off the south face, I am greeted by an icy snow-laden gale and a headlong view four thousand feet down Mount Kenya's opposite north side. The Gate of the Mists is a knife-edge, literally no wider than a gate. The contrast between the South Face I've just come from and the North Face is shocking. In the space of a few feet the temperature difference seems thirty degrees. The North Face spreads out below in deep shadow, encrusted from top to bottom with ice and snow. It is truly in the midst of winter.

By contrast, Harley's mood has changed from winter to warm. He grasps my mittened hand in both his and yanks it up and down, slapping me on the back and howling above the wind,

"Well, we made it, laddie!" He is all smiles, as effervescent as champagne. Grasping the pack from my back, he slings it over his shoulder and gestures up. "Come on—the summit!"

He bounds away, quickly climbing up the small rocky pyramid. The summit lies but another hundred feet above us. I follow after, excited. My brain has now given up registering the repetitive kick-step-up-rest, kick-step-up-rest movements of my body. It is free to wander. To relive the day's events. As in a slide projector, only much faster, the images flash across my mind: Harley on the initial ice dagger, he and I moving in unison up the narrow chute of the Couloir, the forbidding expanse of the upper headwall, lunch at our airy perch, all of Africa spread at our feet. They are imprints caught for eternity.

We take the final steps to the summit. I pull myself back to the immediate, pushing all other thoughts out of mind. There will be time enough for them later. Together we stand on Africa's second-highest peak watching the sun, a dying ember, sink beneath us into the horizon.

The following afternoon, after Harley and I are safely descended off the mountain, the Diamond Ice Couloir avalanches. A fallen icicle, a tumbling stone, it is sudden; no one sees how it starts. The entire face lets loose, a hundred thousand tons of snow. It roars and rumbles down from the Gate of the Mists over the headwall and into the Couloir, finally spilling onto the talis slope at the bottom at over 150 miles an hour. The noise is deafening. It lasts maybe thirty seconds. But in that time the entire South Face is scoured clean—down to bedrock and black ice. Not a patch of snow remains.

We are dead on our feet by the time we are back at the hut, two doddering old men, full of cricks and palsy. It was a long, cold, tiring night on the summit—with one bivy sack between us. The effects of the altitude have finally caught up with us. Immediately Harley disappears within the depths of his sleeping bag. I prop myself up against a boulder and try to doze in the sunshine. My mind races. The twisting, tumbling finality of this morning's avalanche replays itself in my brain. The consequences. If we had climbed one day later, Harley and I would be dead now. But we weren't! That's the thing. We had made the climb, and in good style. We worked and climbed together as a team under conditions as trying and difficult as any for success. This unto itself was something to be pleased about. In retrospect the problems between us seem slight considering the circumstances. During the descent this morning, Harley explained to me that the altitude had gotten to him yesterday, making him weak, nauseous. He had gone too high too fast. If such was the case, he is all the more remarkable to have performed as well as he did. There should be no such problem on Kili. The approach spans a number of days, rising gradually in altitude. We will be perfectly acclimatized by the time we reach the Breach Wall. And for this wall, more and more I sense Harley will be an ideal companion. What he lacks in experience and judgment (really his only weakness) he more than makes up for in technical expertise, resolve, and strength. More important, he is open-minded even if moody—as he has just proven on the Diamond Ice Couloir—and ultimately will listen to reason.

With a little luck and conditions better than we've had on Mount Kenya, we should achieve a similar success on Kilimanjaro's Breach Wall. I am certain of it.

Harley is still in his sleeping bag when I set off the next morning for a hike toward the West Face. I move rapidly, stretching with each step, trying to work out the kinks in my aching body. Halfway there, I see two black dots gliding rapidly down the shimmering surface of the glacier, which reflects so much light it hurts my eyes to look at them. They appear no bigger than mites in a drift of snow. I alter my course and head toward them. Thirty minutes later I recognize the two Ians. They are burned black by the sun save for gaunt white eye sockets left untanned under the shield of their goggles. They are exuberant—having been successful with the buttress—and at the same time relieved to see me, having witnessed the avalanche in the Couloir. They thought we were goners for sure. I assure them that all is well, telling them of our success as we head back toward the hut.

Harley lounges drowsily in the sun on the stone step leading into the hut, his fully packed rucksack beside him.

"You're all set for another route already?" asks Iain Allen, raising his eyebrows in exaggerated awe. "What will it be now? Point John? The West Face?" Iain winks knowingly to Ian and me.

"No," answers Harley, "I'm going down. I'm finished with Mount Kenya."

"What about your four other routes?" Iain is unable to keep a straight face any longer.

"Some other time," says Harley, breaking into a thin grin now as well. "I'm through with this snow-slogging. I'm up for some steep dry rock and sun. Come on! Hurry up and get a drink. Let's go."

In five minutes' time we are off at a near-trot, Harley leading the way down the mountain. Down to ice-cold beer, pints of shandy, and disappointment. The border between Kenya and Tanzania has been closed, and with it our access to Kilimanjaro.

VI

Have you heard the children crying?
Have you seen the blood-stained streets?
Have you realized men are dying
And ever wondered why?

Down below, the screams and staccato rifle fire erupt once more from the night-shrouded streets of Addis Ababa. In the not-too-remote distance mortar shells pepper some unseen adversary. In silence, Harley and I listen to the dull repetitive thud as round after round is discharged, each followed seconds later by a sharper, more resonant explosion as the shell impacts. Ethiopia. A country under siege. There is no question we have made a mistake coming here. But who was to know it would be like this? Now all we can do is wait and hope—and get out as soon as possible.

It is difficult to imagine now that only days ago Harley and I stood together on Mount Kenya's summit watching the sunset. It was beautiful, so peaceful we could catch each other's thoughts without speaking, so quiet we could almost hear the clouds roll by. A strange circuitous journey has brought us here from that place on high. This is another world, another time.

It began in the last century during the reign of Queen Victoria when Africa's two greatest peaks, Kenya and Kilimanjaro, lay within the British East African Crown Colony. To the south and west were the lands of the royal German colony called Tanganyika. The two were continually at odds, with no defined borders to separate them. In 1886 a treaty was enacted by Britain and Germany to delineate permanent boundaries. It was during this time, on the birthday of her German grandson, Wilhelm, that Victoria presented Kilimanjaro to him as a gift and a show of good faith. With the sweep of her pen, boundaries were obliterated and redrawn, and Kilimanjaro shifted from Britain to Germany. Close to eighty years later these East African colonies achieved their independence, the British land becoming the nation of Kenya, the German land becoming Tanzania. The boundary separating them stood unchanged, however, with Kilimanjaro a mere twelve miles inside Tanzania from the Kenyan border. Subsequently the two nations took very different political directions: Kenya under Kenyatta became a capitalist stronghold, while Tanzania under Nyerere assumed a socialist stance, leaning toward Communism. Now, in 1978, things had come to a head between the two countries, each accusing the other of gross improprieties, of economic sabotage, of raiding and stealing cattle, and of failure to uphold and support the cooperative of East African States. Overnight all communication and ties were severed and the borders sealed between Kenya and Tanzania. The only option open for Harley and me was to travel to a third, neutral country to pass between the two. As we soon found out, this was easier said than done. Africa is a continent of nations at odds. Uganda was open from Kenya, but closed to Tanzania. Zambia was open to Tanzania, but closed from Kenya. Zaire, Mozambique, Rhodesia were all closed to and from both. In the end the only logical and perhaps only possible choice was Ethiopia. It was accessible to both countries, and on a daily basis. We booked our flights, realizing full well we would now travel more than 1,500 miles to cover the 250-mile distance to Kilimanjaro, but we had no choice.

At the crack of dawn, January 9, Harley and I were back at Nairobi International Airport saying our goodbyes to Iain. We had a 7:10 A.M. flight out to Addis Ababa. I felt sad leaving. It seemed we had only just arrived. In reality, we had been there a little more than a week. This was too short, too rushed a trip for me. We had come half way round the world. Who knew when we'd get back this way again? Nevertheless, our major objective in Africa, our reason for coming, the Breach Wall, remained. And daily now Harley's pressing business commitments in the States—sales meetings in Los Angeles, trade shows in Texas, movie contracts in New York—all grew closer and more urgent. He had few days left for Africa. I would miss Iain and his dry humor. I had even invited him along to Kili, an idea Harley was less than keen on. Eager as Iain was to join us, he told me Tanzania was no place for a Kenyan just now. There was always a chance his presence might jeopardize our entire trip. "Next time. For sure!" he said, turning to depart. Stamped through passport control, I yelled back to him that perhaps I would see him after the Kili climb. He broke into a broad grin, gave me the thumbs-up sign.

Seven A.M. rolled around, and the crowded disembarkation lounge at Nairobi International grew restless. There was no sign of an Ethiopian jet on the runway, yet Indians, Arabs, blacks and Malaysians began moving toward the single exit. It appeared that Harley and I were the only whites on the flight. We watched with amusement from our lounge chairs as everyone jockeyed for position. It was all done subtly at first, but soon all decorum was abandoned. They pushed, shoved and heaved at each other. In minutes they were squeezed into a tightly knotted ball, a weaving mass of arms and legs similar to a scrum in a rugby match, only much larger. In fact, in complete contrast to rugby, there appeared to be no limit to the number of players or replacements. Passenger after passenger continued to join the melee. With each addition we found it all the more hilarious. Unlike any simple game, there were no winners here; occasionally an individual might attain the prized portal position for a moment or two, but he soon lost it. Nor was there any time limit on the action. It was well past 8 A.M. now; obviously the flight was delayed, still the jousting continued, every man fighting for a position in line for nothing.

By 10:30 the smug smiles had been wiped from our faces. There came an announcement. The flight was indefinitely delayed due to an emergency in the north; our plane had been diverted to carry troops to the area. Harley and I could only guess the message's meaning. A riot? A revolt? There was no war in Ethiopia as far as we knew. None that NBC, BBC, or *Time* had reported. The estimated arrival time of the flight in Nairobi was now late afternoon or early evening. We would wait.

And wait we did. The hours passed. We slouched and slept, sat and read. At times I watched, in awe, as Indian and Pakistani peddlers carried on a rigorous black-market business of buying and selling passenger vouchers. The airport had just issued food and drink, which immediately became part of the bustling economic activity. I marveled at them, age-old instant entrepreneurs. Buy. Sell. Barter. It was all they knew—passed down the centuries to them. It ran in their veins like blood. All the while still more people bunched into the corner by the portal, though not nearly so fervently now. Most had dropped onto the floor and lay prostrate, asleep or guarding over their belongings. There were probably four to five hundred people. How could all of them be booked on a single plane, even a jumbo jet?

Midafternoon I had my answer. The roar of jet engines, and suddenly a plane squeaked to a stop before the gateway. A bold red ETHIOPIAN AIRWAYS spread out on the fuselage. It had actually come, and the terminal had noisily come to life once more. "Boarding for Flight 031 in ten minutes." How could all these people fit on a single 707? There would never be enough seats. I glanced down at our tickets to check the flight number. It corresponded. Then suddenly I realized we had no seat assignments. I ran off to the airline counter. Impatiently awaiting my turn in line, I could scarcely believe my ears. They were still selling tickets on today's Flight 031 for Addis Ababa. When my turn arrived I explained to the counter attendant there had been a mistake. We had waited all day. My tickets were missing seat-assignment numbers. She stared straight into my eyes and icily said, "There's been no mistake. Ethiopia is a *socialist* country. There are no assigned seats. It's open. First come, first served." She spurned me with a kind of sarcastic half-smile and said, "Better hurry up and get in line." Suddenly it all made sense. The crowd. The pushing. The shoving. I raced back to Harley and explained. We threw ourselves into the midst of the fray with a vengeance.

The jet was filled, without a glimmer of hope for us. Nine hours' waiting for nothing. Harley was furious. I was depressed. Suddenly a second jet appeared. Another Ethiopian Airways plane. In full fury the pushing and shoving resumed once more. Harley and I locked arms to stick together. Under the crush of flailing bodies, word soon came to us that flight 031 to Addis Ababa had been canceled. All flights to Ethiopia had been suspended indefinitely. Ethiopia had broken its air treaty with Kenya, the treaty which states that only one Ethiopian plane may be in Kenyan air space at one time. Presently there were two, and this could very easily be construed as an act of war. The two planes would be impounded and relations severed until proper reparations were made. Dejectedly Harley and I settled back into our seats to cool our heels once more. Kilimanjaro seemed as far away as the moon, and about as accessible.

An hour passed, perhaps more, then we were inexplicably loaded onto the Ethiopian Airways jet. No announcements were made, no explanations given. By 4 P.M. we were airborne, heading due north.

When we stepped from plane to runway at Emperor Haile Selassie Memorial Airport, we knew something was amiss. A phalanx of machine-gun-toting soldiers, maybe fifty in all, stood at the foot of the gangway at the ready. On all sides the airport was bordered by great round brown hills, a stark contrast to the lush greens of Kenya. Off to the left far down the runway stood transport after gleaming transport, too many to count. Even at this distance one could easily see the hammer and sickle of the Soviet Union on their tails. Before the planes stood what seemed a thousand men ordered into neat columns. Most were troops in green fatigues, a strangely colored uniform, I thought, for an arid, desert-hued country like Ethiopia. A smaller number were dressed in brown. When our flight emptied, fifty troops surrounded us and moved us en masse into the terminal. Harley and I walked in silence, eyes leveled straight ahead as if we saw nothing. From the outside, the terminal was structurally futuristic, with curving, ultramodern lines. Within, it was but an empty shell, exposed crumbling cement, naked bulbs and wires. Customs and immigration brought more of the same joyless reception. A small dark man with a bushy mustache, looking more Arab than African, interrogated us. What were we doing in Ethiopia? Why had we come? Did we know how long we would stay? Where would we stay? I explained our intent as transit travelers, and he gave us a twenty-four-hour entrance visa to Ethiopia costing twenty dollars. That was exactly how he wanted it, in twenty United States dollars. He took our passports and travel documents, saying, "The city is under martial law. That means anyone out after dusk is shot on sight. Go to your hotel and stay there. Tomorrow morning be here at nine A.M. I will give these back to you then." He turned away from us and tossed our passports into a large black box sitting on the floor across the room. Perhaps three feet high, the box was three-quarters filled with travel documents and passports of every shape, size and color, all haphazardly thrown together. At the currency-exchange counter Harley suggested that only he change money. It would be a waste for both of us to do so, and I had absorbed most of the Kenya expenses. We would be here in Ethiopia less than twenty-four hours, and all Ethiopian currency could be confiscated upon our leaving. I agreed, and went off to collect our gear.

The pneumatic gliding doors leading out of the terminal were not working. We had to pry them apart and block them open with our bodies. We passed our sacks through the gap we created and then heaved our bodies out before the doors came crashing closed once again. Outside, we were instantly set upon by a multitude of outstretched hands. In a blur of noise and motion, voices were raised in disjointed Italian crescendo: *"Avanzare! Avanzare! Avanzare!"* When we refused their offers of assistance with "No, thanks. No! No, thank you," immediately their cries shifted to "Mih-yelpa. Mih-yelpa. Mih-yelpa." Harley and I made our way through the throng in search of a taxi while pawing overzealous hands grabbed at our sacks, trying to wrench them away and carry them for us. Finally we found a cab for hire, an ancient gray Fiat, no doubt a World War II remnant. One at a time we tossed our sacks onto the roof rack. Suddenly a small swarthy Ethiopian raced from the crowd and stripped Harley of his great blue pack. It happened so fast there was no time to react. The pack appeared to be almost the same size as the man. With all his might he twisted it over his head, trying desperately to launch it up onto the roof. He was obviously more in pursuit of a tip than of the bag. It tottered wildly in the air a moment, then came crashing down on top of him, knocking him to the dusty roadside. Instantly Harley was upon him. For a moment, from the look of fury on Harley's face, I thought he might punch the man out. He didn't, instead lifting the sack off the pinned man and tossing it onto the roof rack without word or wasted motion, letting his anger stay in his eyes. Quickly we jumped in and the cab raced away from curbside, kicking up a spray of dirt. Out the oval rear window I saw the would-be porter get up and chase after us, shaking his fist. Enrobed in the swirling dust trail of our vehicle, he screamed the vengeance of Allah upon us. Our driver laughed, "Athole."

The trip from airport to city took only fifteen minutes on roadways almost free of civilian traffic. We did pass several columns of military vehicles rumbling out of the city due north.

The streets were lined with people, some tan, some brown, some black, most uniformly dressed in flowing djellabas. The baggy ill-defined lines of the robes obscured any hint of what the people may have looked like. But the rifles slung over their shoulders and the long curved daggers, called jambiyyas, tucked into their belts gave a clear indication of their intent. They were not to be fooled with. When we were stopped at an intersection, Harley thought to take a picture.

Beside us stood a tall, statuesque figure cloaked in white, rifle in hand, two shiny ammunition belts crossing his chest in perfect symmetry. Our driver had only to hear the snap of Harley's camera case and he spun around. "No! No cam-ra! No cam-ra!" His bloodshot eyes were filled with fear. Harley resnapped the case and dropped it to the floor. In five minutes' time we were at our hotel checking in.

It was obvious the Wabe Shebelle had at one time been a luxury hotel; but now, like much of what little we had seen in Ethiopia, it was in a state of dilapidation and decay: curling, threadbare red carpets, peeling paint, de-laminating woodwork. Still, it was only for one night. The desk clerk reiterated the warnings of the immigration officer. It was not safe to wander outside the hotel and forbidden after dusk. We were to keep both sets of shades drawn at all times and stay away from the windows. If we wanted a taxi we needn't search for one, they would get one for us. Harley and I went up to our third-floor room without knowing exactly what to expect. The room was huge, twice the size of a normal hotel room, and mostly empty, save for the two beds in it. Peeking out from behind the doubly draped curtains, we could see down on the crowded streets below. We had an excellent view of this part of the city, as most of the buildings surrounding the hotel were single story, surfaced in light-beige plaster.

In the next few minutes as we unpacked for the evening I realized that my immunization book was missing. In Third World countries this yellow book is more important than a passport. It certifies that the holder is properly immunized against the many dangerous communicable diseases such as typhus, diphtheria, smallpox, or cholera, and is not a carrier. Whereas a passport could be replaced quickly by a government consulate or embassy office, only the original treating physician could reissue an immunization book based on his records, which, considering the present situation here in Ethiopia, might take weeks. In the meantime my entrance to every country in the world, including even the United States or the United Kingdom, would be barred. Without the yellow book one became persona non grata until proven otherwise. I searched each of our packs. No luck. I knew I had the immunization booklet when I left Kenya. After that I wasn't sure. Had I dropped it on the plane? Perhaps at the airport? Had immigration mistakenly taken it? Had the book been stolen outside the terminal in all the confusion? I hadn't the vaguest idea. I decided to go back out to the airport immediately. It was 5:30 P.M., so I had just enough time to get there and back before dusk.

Harley was lying on his bed face down when I told him I needed some money for a taxi. He turned over and matter-of-factly said, "You can't have any. You lost your immunization book through your own fault. If it is gone you will just have to suffer the consequences. It'll make you more careful next time. I'm not going to waste good money now on a useless trip out to the airport and back again. If your immunization papers are there now, they will be there tomorrow."

What the hell was going on? Harley was treating me as if I had planned the entire day's frustration for him. No matter how I tried to explain the ramifications of the effect my book's absence might have upon our trip to Kili—namely, that I couldn't even get into Tanzania—he would not listen. He remained unmoved, saying, "I'm all set and leaving tomorrow morning for Tanzania. I have my immunization booklet." He rolled over and turned his back to me. It was finished as far as he was concerned. He refused to discuss it further.

*   *   *

In the intervening hours of night, I have played back the recent events on the tape of my memory. Harley was angry—at the long delays, at Ethiopia, at the wasted time in general in Africa, and at me for my absentmindedness. People or things which promised one thing but did not live up to expectation were intolerable to Harley. He could not fit them into his ordered, stark view of the world. In disappointment or frustration he was not amenable or accommodating but all the more rigidly steadfast. It was these very qualities that had carried him to the peak in his climbing and in his business; but I sought other peaks. If Harley had lost his immunization papers, I would have felt as bad for him as for myself. It would have been an obstacle to overcome together.

I listen now once more to the night sounds from the street below. There are sporadic bursts of machine-gun fire. A dog is barking. A child cries. In a distance there are screams and sobbing. All intermingled with the whine of snipers' bullets. How many people would die tonight, I wonder? Suddenly I am sad. We have come to a land of death, and below plays its music. I sense a presence in this place. It turns neighbors into adversaries. Man against man. Friend into foe. It is happening to Harley and me.

I waken the next morning having slept badly. Harley is already up and dressed. Camera in hand, he peeks out from the heavy draperies down onto the streets. There is still scattered gunfire, but it is much diminished now.

"This is incredible, Rob!" he whispers to me. "You have to see it!"

He deftly parts material with the snout of his telephoto lens and clicks away, exposure after exposure. Suddenly he stops and steps back. He freezes motionless, holding his breath. I am tempted to say something but hold my tongue. The tense moment passes. He changes his position in the room and resumes shooting. Nervously he whispers to me between shots, "You see those planes yesterday—and the troops? They were Russian or Cuban. Communist anyway. We are in the middle of a war here, and no one even knows it exists yet. Just imagine what the first pictures of it will be worth, in a week's time when it breaks open worldwide. *Time* and *Newsweek* would pay thousands for them."

I leave Harley to his picture taking and go downstairs to request a cab.

The driver is waiting for us in the lobby when we come down twenty minutes later. He is a smiling, good-natured great bear of a man who looks remarkably like Gamal Abdel Nasser, the late President of Egypt, and remarkably bears the same name. He takes a pack from each of us and escorts us out of the hotel. Harley and I stick close to his side as he pushes his way through the milling mob. Every eye in the crowd turns on us as we negotiate the hundred yards to the cab. They stare us up and down. I feel naked, intruded on by the boldness of their stares. It is a relief when we reach a deep-blue '57 Mercedes-Benz. It is in mint condition, not a scratch or particle of dust on it.

Nasser smiles. "Hi wush it evary day," he says, patting the brilliant chrome radiator grill like a proud parent.

We heave our gear into the trunk and jump in. The interior is just as immaculate—glove leather upholstery, even Arabian belly-dancing music playing on the stereo.

Immediately I tell him, "We want to go to the airport. We must be there by nine o'clock."

Nasser looks at the small circular clock in the walnut dash and smiles. "Hate-viftin. Shura. No prahplum."

"No! No! No! Wait a second," Harley interrupts, "we're not going to rush out to the airport. I want to take a drive around— see the sights of Addis. There's no hurry! Nasser, take fifteen to twenty minutes and show me the city."

I am furious. "Harley, you know I want to get out to the airport! We are supposed to be there by nine o'clock, anyway."

Harley laughs, rolling his eyes up to the cab ceiling, then looks me straight in the eye, saying, "Look! Who's paying for this cab, Rob? You know what you can do if you don't like it."

After our tour of the city we are out at the airport by 9:30. I am still boiling mad, but not enough to forget my final glimpses of Addis Ababa: bodies piled upon the sidewalks, great blotches of blood being hosed from roadways down sewer holes. People line the streets armed to the teeth with daggers, swords, rifles, and pistols. Grim reminders of man's inhumanity.

Separately, Harley and I pass through immigration. I hand in my visa card to the clerk. Is it there? I wonder. What will I do if it isn't? He retreats from the counter to the big black box. He fishes out my passport and returns. Fingers wet with perspiration, I check my book. It is not there! I tell the clerk I am missing something—my yellow book. Grudgingly, once again he returns to the box. He rifles through the many books and documents. A minute's searching . . . and he lifts it out. I pass on, book in hand, to join a waiting Harley.

"Happy now?" he snickers. "I knew it was there all the time! What a worry wart. I hope that taught you a good lesson for the future. Now come on, let's go get a drink."

He heads up the stairs to the departure lounge. I am so relieved, my anger has dissipated. Still, as I climb the stairs I find myself questioning what he means about "a good lesson."

Our 9:30 flight to Tanzania is soon delayed to noon. "Emergency on the front!" we are told. Then it is delayed to 1 P.M. Then to 3. Finally at 5 P.M. we prepare to board. Women are directed to the left, men to the right. Each passenger must pass through one of two large gray-curtained cubicles before exiting to the waiting jet. A dozen gun-ready soldiers oversee the operation. When it is my turn, I enter the cubicle. Within, a pistol-toting officer directs me to hoist my shirt up to my armpits and hold it there. He drops my trousers and shorts, then bends me over forward for a good look. It takes but seconds and the inspection is over. I only wonder what contraband he was searching for.

It is dusk as I walk the short distance to the plane. The sun has long since set, yet the brown hills surrounding the airport still glow a burgundy red. I mount the wobbling metal steps of the gangway and haul up on the dented tubular rail. I cannot be away from this country too soon.

VII

How shall we bridge
The void between us
Now that we have grown apart

The operator tries the number again. I cradle the receiver in the crook of my neck, letting it rest on my shoulder, which is numb from hunched inactivity. I stare down at the once crisp and white business card in my hand. It is grimy, creased, rat-eared now after hours of sweaty-palmed fidgeting. The printing on it seems almost too professional to have been done here—some artifact of Europe perhaps, alien to the style of Africa, at least what I have seen of it thus far. It reads:

ODD ELIASSEN
KILIMANJARO NATIONAL PARK
TEL. MARANGU 50

Through the crackle of static I hear the operator say, "Hit-yor numma ring."

"It's actually ringing!" I yell excitedly from the phone booth across to the slumped figure beneath the banana bush.

Since our arrival at Kilimanjaro Airport in Tanzania late last night, over twelve hours behind schedule, we have begun a succession of calls attempting to reach Odd, who lives in Marangu on the northern shoulder of Kilimanjaro. We tried first at the airport, then in town at Arusha, and lastly at a hostel in

Moshi where we ended up spending the night, having run out of energy and choices at such a late hour. As our Tanzanian contact, Odd is pivotal to our plans, for he can provide us with information on mountain conditions, local weather, and various approaches, clueing us in on any other exotic peculiarities of the Kilimanjaro area. Though neither Harley nor I know him personally, we are aware of his worldwide reputation as an alpinist. A Norwegian, Odd has been living on Mount Kiliman-jaro over the past several years, working for the Tanzanian National Park System. Norwegian friends have told us that Odd has developed a knowledge of Kili few men can match, an instinctive familiarity that comes only from living in a place for years. It is in fact through these friends that Odd knows of and is now expecting us. It was all arranged—only the exact date of our arrival was not fixed. Obviously, after the past days' experiences, we realize why such a thing is impossible to know in Africa.

The operator returns. "Surrimista—el-E-a-sin nut dare!" Click.

"Hello! Hello! Helooo! Damn! Cut off again." I slash the receiver at the phone box in anger. Harley emits a small laugh from his supine position, but he is not smiling. It is a sign of futility. Ethiopia, the hassles, the frustrations of the past few days have worn on both of us. It is reflected in our relationship. From our time in Addis to now, there has been a tension between us. We scarcely talk to each other. The close kinship of Mount Kenya is but a memory now. The only hope of restoration is to get away from these places of men and their conflicts. We must go to the mountains. We are within striking distance of our objective now—Kili rises up before us less than fifty miles away. Yet we are frustrated once again. I am out of patience and out of change for another call.

"What do you think we should do?" I ask.

"Well, it's obvious the phone's not the answer. It's given us nothing for all the time, effort, and money we've put into it."

"How about if we just make the trip over to Marangu and look Odd up? It can't be that far."

"Rob! It's seventy kilometers from here—the opposite direction from where we wanna go. Besides, we'd have to take a bus. That shoots today, tomorrow, and probably any chances of doing the climb. Remember, I'm leaving next Thursday. The two extra days could make all the difference to us between success or failure. I say we head off right now and forget about Odd. We can always see him on the way out—after we've climbed the route—if we still have time. You're in no hurry anyway, you can stick around as long as you like."

"But we don't know a thing about—"

He cuts me off in midsentence, chopping the air with his hand. "Listen, Rob. We've got all we need to know to go, from the two Ians. How to get to Umbwe. How to approach the Breach Wall. Now I've got six, maybe seven days left to give to this mountain. Do you want to do this climb or do you want to go see Odd and kiss the climb goodbye? You've gotta make a decision. Either we quit this frigging around and get moving to the mountain or I'm heading back to the airport now for the next flight out. Decide."

I sag against the phone booth in silence, weighing the arguments for and against going. We really don't know a great deal about Kilimanjaro. Oh, we've read about it and looked at maps, and we know how to get from point A to point B, but that's all. We have no experience with this mountain, nor do we know what to expect from it. On the other hand, we have just climbed Mount Kenya and done a good job of it. Certainly Kenya and Kili must be vaguely similar, being only several hundred miles apart. And the two faces do have similar exposures. Moreover, the most critical part of the climb, the upper wall, has never been done successfully. We would have to respond to it rather than pattern our movements after other climbers or their advice.

Still, I have one major misgiving: our attitude toward climbing Kili—giving the mountain only six of seven days. One simply does not approach, climb, and descend a mountain by a rigid schedule. There is enough pressure in the climb itself without adding self-imposed time limits. This is particularly true of a new route on a twenty-thousand-foot mountain. A mountain must be met on its own terms, in its own time, not man's. Yet we've come more than nine thousand miles expressly for this Breach Wall. Now it waits. This will be my only chance. If I hesitate, the opportunity will be gone, perhaps for good. Gone as well would be any chance of my continued climbing with Harley. Did I want that to happen? After several minutes I make my decision. "OK, Harley, let's give it a go."

"At last, Rob, you've come to your senses," he says and smiles, the tension broken.

In a small clearing we stop before a border of sorts. The domesticating influence of man, in open pastures and fields, now yields before the dense, vegetated domain of the jungle. It is an imaginary boundary, marking two distinct, separate worlds. Before setting off we divvy up the gear so as to have equal loads, and make the final adjustments to our small overstuffed packs. Harley takes the eleven-millimeter orange rope, I take the nine-millimeter red one and the ice screws. He takes the gas stove, the cheese and the nuts; I take gas cartridges, soup, cornmeal, and dates. Over the next week our diet will be very boring but at least nutritious. Every day, three times a day, we shall have the same repetitive meal: soup with polenta, some cheese for protein, dates and nuts for between-meal snacks. The need for such a limited menu comes down to simple weight and space efficiency. On this remote southwest side of the mountain, we will have to travel several days through dense jungle and rain forests before having even a glimpse of the Breach Wall. We will trek over fifty miles, going from four thousand feet to over nineteen thousand feet. During the course of our journey temperatures will range from 100 degrees plus at the jungle base to minus 20 degrees at Kili's summit, and we must carry the gear and supplies essential for survival in both extremes. Every ounce must be counted, every square inch of space put to utmost use. To take too little is to court disaster. To take too much will weigh us down and wear us out on the approach.

As cautious as we are in packing, our packs are soon crammed to overflowing—bits and pieces of gear, ropes, jackets, pitons are strung and dangled from sides, top, and back. We complete our preparations by examining the rudimentary map and instructions Iain Allen has traced out for us on the back of a used loose-leaf sheet, detailing the path up the Umbwe Ridge, a long circuitous trail on the western side of Kilimanjaro. "It is often obscured and overgrown in its lower reaches by the jungle. Don't lose heart," his directions say, "Forge ahead, keeping in mind that the ridge falls on an east-west line. Stay in line with the sun and eventually you'll link up with the ridge." It is not a lot to go on, but it gives us a realistic beginning.

We shoulder our shifting loads and head into the shadow cast by the dense ceiling of vegetation overhead. Side by side we begin together, groping our way up the trail, a six-inch gap between two bushes, a slight crimp in waist-high weeds, a dimpled depression in the black peaty mud. It is not so much a path we follow as our intuition. Occasionally we wander wrong, fetching up dead-ended by the trunk of a tree or an impenetrable thicket. But we reverse ourselves and soon right our course. At times hardly a trace of sky is visible through the tangle of branches and leaves enveloping us. So much for following the line of the sun. Yet somehow there is enough light for a rich undergrowth to survive. It is dotted by an endless assortment of wildflowers, yellow trumpets, red stars, purple balls, bluebells, each as unique and striking as the next. Occasionally we stop to take photos, but there is simply not enough light. Onward we hike in the shade. Neither Harley nor I have been in an equatorial country before, so this jungle mountaineering offers us a new experience. The flowers, the gnarled knotted vines, the lush vegetation all surround and lean down on us in an overbearing, almost threatening sort of way. These plants are the powerful life force here, and they appear to grow before my eyes. I sense that if one stopped and remained still too long in this place he would be entwined and overpowered, claimed as one of their own. And the silence! The air is quiet—no cawing or whistling birds, no chattering, jumping monkeys, no sound whatsoever except for an occasional soft rustling, its source unseen in the undergrowth. Even mosquitoes are absent. It is as if we have stepped into Eden on the fourth day of creation, while it is still devoid of animal life. Yet there are undeniable signs to the contrary: though we see not a single spider, the narrow pathway through the wood is laced with immense gauzy silks of countless webs that I imagine must have been made by spiders a foot across.

Farther along we observe toothmarked seed pods and several different types of animal droppings. Hoof and paw prints remain etched in the moist black earth. Where are the creatures? The infinite subtlety of jungle life refuses to unfold for us. We can only imagine what the jungle hints at as we traipse blindly through the bush. In this kingdom of quiet we too are quiet as if fearful our speaking will shatter the magical spell of tranquility.

Harley and I gradually drift apart and lose sight of each other as we hike along, each at his own pace, entering the cocoon of solitude common to prolonged mountain trekking. The body engaged in its repetitive routine allows the mind a freedom to wander at will. At one time it drinks in the bush-jungle scenery; at another it is deep in meditation preparing for the upcoming climb. It's funny. Over the years approaches have become as integral a part of alpinism to me as the climbing. The dusty winding path up to the Argentière basin in Chamonix. The prickly poplar thickets and avalanche blowdowns into Robson in the Rockies. The twenty-mile gritty, crevasse-riven glacier access to Djanghi-tau in Russia or the wet sopping bog up to the Ben in Scotland. What to many a climber is painful drudgery, I've grown to look forward to. Every approach is a new experience, yet each shares that moment of peace before the struggle.

Kili's approach is unique. The jungle's mystery begins to seem spooky to me. Where are all those animals people back home said to be careful of? Flashes of old Tarzan movies flick by my mind. I soon find myself glancing back over my shoulder, turning at the mere snap of a twig. I start to imagine such unseen specters as man-eating leopards, venomous black mambas, or the goring horns of cape buffalo just around the next bend through that curtain of young bamboo. Is Harley still behind me—just around that bend, out of sight? I suppress the urge to call out to him, to see if he's there. I know well enough that if any mishap should befall Harley he would let out a holler most of East Africa would hear. When at last the rocky crest of the Umbwe Ridge rises abruptly before me, it is none too soon. I sit beneath a great concave wall of rock, put some water on for tea, and wait for him. After twenty minutes I begin to get concerned. Half an hour later he arrives at a dead run, blanched white as a sheet.

"Bloody hell!" he gasps, tossing his pack to the ground and collapsing onto it. "I was back maybe two hundred yards or so, kneeling over, shooting some flowers. All of a sudden, right behind me, there's this incredible noise, all this thrashing about. I swung round and saw plants moving everywhere, and it wasn't no monkey moving 'em. This thing was huge! I saw its shadow. Whatever it was, it was big."

Unconsciously, I find myself interrogating him. "What did you think it was? Which direction did it go? Did it follow after you?" Meanwhile my brain races for a logical course of action should the unseen and unwanted predator suddenly appear, bounding up the trail behind us. We could run for cover in the bush or shimmy up a tree. No, Iain Allen's advice is best followed. Stay put. We light the stove in front of us, our flanks and rear protected by the curved rock wall. As a last resort we can always throw paper on the stove burner to flame up a fire, something all animals instinctively fear. Tense minutes pass. All remains quiet.

"Ya know, Rob, I probably scared that feller as much as he scared me." We laugh, relaxing our guard. Danger has brought us closer together. The past day's stress has vanished. It's a relief. Harley gestures above my head toward the overhung rock wall. It is made of slotted blocks, each stacked perfectly upon the other, looking almost like a halved igloo except that the rock is black. From every crack and crevice water oozes, dribbling off the roof's lip into space.

"This must be the first cave Iain spoke of," says Harley. "We're making good time."

"What an ungodly place to spend the night."

"I couldn't agree more. This is where he and his clients were set upon by a leopard. Iain had to keep the fire going all night long to keep the cat at bay—until dawn when the sunlight forced it into its den."

"Do you think that's what you glimpsed?"

"Who knows? Maybe. This is the spot those two Dutch fellows got it, too."

"Got what?"

"No one knows. They just up and vanished, or were carried away. Strange. They left all their gear and food behind, even their tent. A park ranger found the stuff weeks later when the boys were reported overdue. Everything was untouched. And the boys—to this day there's been not a trace of them. They disappeared into thin air."

I swig back my tea and say, "We'd better get moving if we're going to clear this forest by nightfall."

"Sounds good to me. Let's get out of here; this place gives me the creeps."

We climb upward upon the steeply inclined ridge. Within a quarter of a mile we notice the distinct transition from one climatic zone to another. The dense overpowering jungle vegetation which has smothered down upon us all day gives way to openness. Sky at last! The path ahead climbs amidst clumps of immense heather—plants rising ten, fifteen, twenty, even twenty-five feet in the air. It is a forest of heather trees—a heathland gone rampant. We wind our way by and beneath their branches enrobed in Spanish moss. The slender green strands drip from every limb, fluttering idly in the breeze like strange

Christmas-tree decorations. The twisted naked stalks of the heather are more like tree trunks than stems and are host to a spectrum of yellow, red, blue lichens. They cling to us like small grasping animals. The rolling afternoon mists break over the ridge crest like clutching fingers. The landscape resembles some space-monster movie set more than the approach to a mountain climb. At the ten-thousand-foot level the ridge lies back, easing in angle, but makes up for its lack of steepness by becoming a narrow serrated knife-edge scarcely a foot wide in places. Carefully, we clamber up and about slimy, moss-covered, rock towers dotting the ridge like giant twisted shark's teeth. In and out we weave around isolated stalks of rotting heather which have sprouted ever higher in search of life but found only death in this oxygen-starved atmosphere. Ahead the ridge narrows to a sliver of rock so slender my feet must straddle opposite sides of the rock leaf to maintain my balance. Cautiously, arms outstretched, balancing, I move forward on the ridge crest, which is covered by a thin slippery veneer of lichens and alpine plants. On both sides beneath my feet the earth falls away for thousands of feet, nothing but air, down to the plush green carpet of the rain forest. Down to the deafening roar of the Umbwe and Wera-Wera rivers, far below, hidden by the verdant canopy. I have seen greater height, more exposure than this before and been less impressed. It is not the extent of the view but the conditions of it here that are so impressive, unique. In all the thousands of feet that fall vertically away, there is scarcely a square foot of bare rock exposed. The walls are swathed in green, with vines, trees, bushes, plants, flowers—even the undercuts and overhangs wear a shroud of plants. I edge forward, three-thousand feet of space to the jungle below. I grow intoxicated by this jungle mountaineering.

A mile more of this high-wire maneuvering and we arrive at the point where the ridge end joins up with the main bulk of the mountain. In only one hundred yards our path strikingly changes from razor-backed ridge to broad, almost level plateau. We are slowed now as the day's exertion under heavy loads and our lack of acclimatization—we've gained eight thousand feet in altitude today—catch up with us. We stumble along the plateau spread out before us, searching for a good bivouac, stopping in the first meadow with a spring, under the shelter of an enormous concave boulder. We say little, partially out of weariness, but also because there is no need. Each step up the mountain has brought a greater harmony to our movements. Harley prepares the campsite. I put on the soup for supper and watch the sun sink below the horizon. Its rays filtered by the oblique angle, it sets a burnished orange, squashed into an oval. Beneath us now lies the Umbwe Ridge, like some colossal spiky prehistoric creature's tail. I stare down its length as it drops out of sight into the darkness of night. Above, the rest of the beast remains hidden in the mist. Today we have scaled this monster's tail and crept onto its lower back. Tomorrow we shall journey up on its body and the next day mount its ice-crusted head by the Breach Wall. It is difficult to comprehend the sheer immensity of this creature, Kilimanjaro. Settling in for the night, Harley and I simultaneously heave sighs of relief. We can rest peacefully knowing that the jungle and its hidden, lurking dangers now lie far below. We are comfortable and safe here.

In climbing, "alpine starts" are a way of life. Under the frosty darkness of early morning the alpinist arises before the sun to prepare himself for the day's outing. With the first light, often even before, he is away from his bivouac, taking full advantage of the precious hours of daylight. For Harley and me on this second morning of approach, our well-intentioned "alpine start" fails to materialize. Nestled deep within my sleeping bag to ward off the chill of night, I am not conscious for a long while of the sun's warm glow upon my face. Eventually the rays of orange light filter through. It's light out! What time is it? I unzip my sleeping bag and roll to my knees, then slowly to my feet. Above ten thousand feet one simply doesn't go jumping up. The blood all too quickly drains from your head, leaving you oxygen-starved, and you pass out. I check the time. "A quarter to nine! Come on, Harley, get up! We've already missed two and a half hours of daylight."

He grumbles and then rolls over to fend me off a few minutes longer. It is indeed late. Not even a trace remains of last night's hard frost in our little meadow surrounded by heather. Only scattered droplets of dew endure, tucked behind various lumps of boulders, bushes, and plant leaves in the fading blue shadows of morning.

When Harley drags himself up, he is feeling the altitude. The mere mention of the minestrone soup I've made for breakfast makes him wince. But he is right as rain after four or five cups of fruit tea. Breakfast finished, we frantically repack and by 9:30 are under way, settling once more into the rhythm of hiking, trudging upward at a good pace toward our still elusive, as yet unseen objective. With the night's rest we have recovered from yesterday's exertion, and with the morning's activity we are acclimating well, with barely a symptom of altitude sickness. An hour's time, and another transition of climatic zone takes place. We leave behind the stalky forest of heather and enter into vast open alpine meadows. The sparse ground-hugging vegetation brings back fond memories of the Highland moors of Scotland, bleak, desolate, yet exuding a wild, savage beauty. However, these high-altitude meadows are studded with strange, enormous plants. At first I mistake them for saguaro or barrel cacti, but upon closer inspection I find them to be giant African versions of some very common American wildflowers, groundsels and lobelias, weeds really. The giant groundsel rises up to twenty feet on its rubbery, twisted brown stem to a great round ball of green waxy leaves. The giant lobelia is a pale-green tube covered from top to bottom with wispy hairlike leaves which flutter in the slightest breeze. Under unique conditions upon the flanks of Kilimanjaro these plants have mutated and flourished into a species many times the size of their North American counterparts. Kilimanjaro has no end of surprises in store for us.

Onward we hike through the wondrous meadows. The plateau's earlier open gentleness becomes conspicuously rumpled and more hilly. It is difficult to imagine how so many worlds can be encompassed on a single mountain's side: ridges, ravines, jungles, rain forests, gorges, plains, meadows; and each is intriguing enough to merit its own exploration anywhere else in the world, but here on Kilimanjaro individual identities are lost in the mountain's hugeness. We skirt leftward around the side of a large grassy hummock.

Suddenly, there in the distance, rising up in front of us, is the Breach Wall, a great gash in the uniformity of Kilimanjaro's side. Though still two days' march away, there it stands, immense, towering, straining to touch the very sun. The Breach Wall is a study in contrasts, hanging white icefields, shimmering in the morning light, alternating with black vertical cliff bands of rock embellished with the most incredible and unlikely-looking icicles dangling down hundreds of feet. Even at this distance we begin sizing up the face immediately, plotting the path of our prospective route.

"There is no question that's the line to do," says Harley. "That icicle in the center straight up to the top!"

Still awestruck, I scrutinize the wall for more detail—we are still too far away.

When I do not respond, Harley comes again, "You don't agree?"

"Well, sure it's the best line on the face. I just hope it's in condition."

"Whaddya mean?" he shoots back. From the tone of his voice I sense that our newfound synergy may once more be in jeopardy.

"Look, I think you're right, but we're still too far away to make a final decision." I try to soothe him with reasoning. "We have no idea what conditions are like up there. We can't know from so many miles away."

"Rob, that icicle is hanging there perfect. Of course it's safe and climbable. Now, I'd like to know what you're trying to get at."

My efforts at peace are to no avail. We begin our verbal jousting in earnest. "I'm not trying to get at anything, Harley. That icicle may well be safe and climbable. I'm not saying it is or isn't—only that we reserve judgment a bit. Let's check out the conditions. Neither you nor I—nor for that matter probably anyone—has done sustained climbing on vertical ice at over nineteen thousand feet before. It is a tremendous proposition. In fact, conditions and timing probably will be the deciding factors in our success or failure."

"Rob, we just pissed up that vertical ice on Mount Kenya," Harley retorts. "Remember? And the Diamond Couloir was hardly in perfect condition. Why all the second thoughts?"

He is not listening, but I give it one last shot. "First, the vertical ice in the Diamond Couloir was at least two thousand feet lower in altitude and about one-quarter the size of that icicle you see on the Breach Wall. Those are tremendous differences. Second, though we certainly had bad conditions in the upper snowfield, the couloir and the ice wall were near-perfect. We timed our arrival just right. One hour later and we wouldn't have gotten up that headwall. One day later and we'd both be dead now."

Harley smiles, then grows serious. "Listen, Rob, I don't know what all this sudden hedging is about, but just hear me out a minute. Whether a difficulty is at nineteen feet above sea level, nineteen hundred feet or nineteen thousand feet, it's all the same problem. It takes the same approach, entails the same methods and techniques to overcome it. There is no difference. Don't go and get all overawed and scared on me now by this mountain like the rest of these African climbers. This mountain is impressive, but this route's going to be a piece of cake for us, just a couple of hundred feet, you'll see. Now come on, let's get going."

We set off, hiking once more in silence. It is good to be moving again. For all the moorland scenery surrounding me, I take in little of it now. Having seen the Breach Wall, I realize it is a prize, a gem, as attractive and desirable as any woman could ever be to a man. Harley and I both want it badly. But the things Harley has said puzzle, no, trouble me. Some of the notions he spouts so assuredly are diametrically opposed to the concepts of mountains and climbing I hold. For Harley and me it is a difference of management versus response. He desires to control, dictate to, and dominate the mountain wall. I prefer to read it out, reacting and adjusting to its personality out of respect for the wall. Yet I cannot help feeling a twinge of self-doubt. Do I disagree with Harley just for what he says, or am I overreacting to his brashness and lack of respect for this mountain? I must at least keep an open mind. I march on.

By the mile we approach closer. The Breach Wall and the great square summit block of Kilimanjaro swell in size above us. I am too absorbed in thought to appreciate it. All the same, we are making fantastic time. It is only eleven in the morning and already we have passed the trail junction marking the end of the Umbwe route. To the left the route breaks off over the Shira Plateau, to the right the path runs down to Horombo. For us it is straight ahead to our kick-off point to the Breach Wall. We are only minutes past the trail junction when the foggy mist first appears. It is sudden, swarming down upon us as if from nowhere. The rushing clouds lap at the base of the Breach Wall, then in an instant puff up and engulf it. The Wall is gone, and with it any chance we have of approaching it today. We have not had the opportunity to closely examine the Wall, nor have we evaluated the possible routes to follow. It would be foolhardy to attempt an approach with all features, all landmarks on the face, obscured. The skies darken and rumble, sending us scurrying for shelter. We make it to the Barranco Bivouac, a small sardine-can affair at thirteen thousand feet, just as the rain comes down. It slashes across the arched tin roof in an ever-growing symphony of hollow, high-pitched pings. "Imagine that," says Harley, his spirits dampened, "only half past eleven and we're stuck here till tomorrow."

"Sure looks that way," I sigh, slumping down onto my sleeping bag.

"What a drag!" says Harley, tossing his sack to the floor and kicking it across the hut.

"Maybe," I say, "but you get used to it. Alpinism is as much a game of waiting as climbing. You've got to do what the weather tells you to do and when it tells you. Expect to be frustrated— you usually won't be disappointed."

Unresigned, Harley counters, "That's fine for you to say. You've got all the time in the world. But do you realize if it's still pissing down tomorrow our attempt on the Breach Wall is finished? There'll be too little time left to start the day after." Once more he brings up his time schedule. If he is trying to instill a feeling of pressured urgency in me, he's doing a good job of it.

Gas stove fired up, the remainder of the day is an endless series of brews. The rain continues outside as we pour down cup after cup of hot tea. Each of us sinks into silent, separate musing. Harley absorbs himself in a battered copy of a November 23, 1977, *Newsweek* he has found on the floor. In only six weeks the magazine has found its way nine thousand miles to this remote spot. The editors would be proud. I can see the ad now: "*Newsweek* scales the heights!"

I scan the ragged hut register wrapped in a soggy old MacVitte's Digestive Biscuit box, finding the familiar names of old friends: "October '77: Doug Scott and Tut Braithwaite. U.K. In to try Breach Wall. No Luck! Soaked to skin for a week." Sounds like this weather is pretty typical here. Let's hope we have better fortune. I turn the page only to see an entry from just last week: "January 3, '78, Bob Barton, Dave Morris—new route on the Heim." Though it followed a line far to the right of our proposed route up the Breach Wall, still this was great news for us. Conditions must be fairly stable if these Scots lads managed a new route only nine days ago. I read on. It is amusing reading some of the more lucid derring-do descriptions of perilous journeys on this remote side of Kilimanjaro. I find the two Ians' names several times, including a lengthy account of the leopard assault that took place in the forest below. I flip through the tattered pages, my mind painting pictures to go with names and exploits written up. Italians, Germans, French, Americans, many nationalities at one time or another have passed this way; but it is obvious from the small size of the register that it is not so often. Idly I sift through the pages, when suddenly my eyes catch a too-familiar name: "Knowles." Dave! I don't believe it! It's Dave Knowles! My eyes rivet to his thin pencil scrawl upon the page. It reads: "August 10, 1971, Dave Knowles. I've come across the Shira Plateau—atrocious weather, rain, sleet, snow, terrible winds. Tomorrow will go across to Mweka then on to Saddle to complete circumvention of Kilimanjaro. Thanks for the hut. As great as my need—is my appreciation." I picture Dave stomping alone across the barren barrancos, leaning into the rain-choked gales. Left hand firmly planted upon the rim of his GI jungle hat, Dave draws it down over his gray eyes to escape the stinging wind-driven droplets. Forward he staunchly marches, red anorak wildly flapping in the tempest, like some half-crazed scarecrow on his solitary journey. The image is he, so true to life, yet also comic. It makes me chuckle, shattering the silence.

"What's so funny?" asks Harley, disturbed from his pensive reading.

"Oh, sorry—I've just discovered that a friend of mine, Dave Knowles, came here and signed in some years ago when he was trying to hike around Kilimanjaro alone."

"Alone? Imagine that crazy bugger! Dave Knowles—sounds familiar. Wasn't he killed somewhere?"

As if I could have forgotten. Harley's words drive the joy from within me. "He was killed on the Eiger by rockfall in '74."

Harley returns to his *Newsweek*. Helplessly I turn to the haunting images of Dave's death. It was the close of the second day's shooting for a spy-mountaineering thriller called *The Eiger Sanction*, filmed on location in the Swiss Alps. Dave and cameraman Mike Hoover had just finished filming the obligatory mountain rock slide sequence complete with Hollywood-style hollow plastic rocks. They stood on their ledge tucked beneath a rock buttress on the Eiger's West Ridge and chatted as they broke down and packed away the camera gear. Theirs was a commanding view down three thousand feet to the green cow pastures of Kleine Scheidegg, now masked in evening shadow beneath the Eiger North Wall. It was a beautiful, peaceful evening. They could even hear the tinkling of cow bells, so calm was it. Now as twilight crept up the valley, Dave felt it was time to move. Where was that damn helicopter to lift them off? They stood side by side, less than an arm's length apart, looking, listening, talking. Dave opened his mouth to speak. Suddenly both of them heard a faint *whirr*ing from above—not the *whirr* of a helicopter, but the whistle of rock fall. Instantly Mike dove into the side, huddling into as small a ball as he could. The ledge exploded in a cloud of flying shards of rock. In seconds all was quiet again. Mike opened his eyes and turned to see Dave at his side. Dave's safety helmet and the top of his head were gone. Death had been instantaneous. So swift, only a trickle of blood oozed from what was left of his head. It was as if the life had been vacuumed out. Even in death Dave's steel-gray eyes bore out at Mike, his pursed lips still holding the word they would never release.

Four thousand miles away it was a sweltering August day. I had just collected the mail. On top of a stack of letters was one from Dave in Switzerland. He was having a grand time, living it up in high Hollywood style. He stood to make a fair bit o' brass on this job—more in a month than he usually cleared in a year. He was anxiously awaiting my arrival in Grindelwald in a week's time. He closed by saying the Canadian Rockies were "on" for this winter. It was an uplifting letter and one that left me keen to join him and leave behind the drudgery of vegetable picking and gardening for a time.

The next letter I opened was a small yellow packet from Western Union. I couldn't imagine what it could be about. Curious, I scanned the first few lines: "DEAR ROB . . . WITH REGRET . . . DEATH . . . DAVE KNOWLES . . . EIGER . . .

ROCKFALL." I could not believe my eyes. I reread the telegram, studying each word. Still I would not believe. Dave's letter in my hand disproved it. It had to be a mistake. One call to Europe, I had my answer. Dave was gone. The very day he had written me, he was killed.

It grows dark within the Barranco Bivouac now. I have been so deep in thought I did not notice the change from day to dusk. The rain continues its patter upon the steel roof. There is little to do but go to sleep and hope for better weather tomorrow. Seven P.M. and Harley and I are sacked out for the long night ahead. As I fall asleep Dave is on my mind and in my dreams.

As knights of the Black Watch, Dave and I proudly wear the blue, black, and red of the clan Stewart in service to our Queen Mary of Scotland. To every corner of the Highlands we bear her royal signet and carry her bidding.

Now under cover of darkness we gallop with urgent news for our Queen. Tomorrow, Friday the thirteenth, the Earl of Moray will attack our forces. Dave and I must raise the alarm. Under pale planting moon we race across the desolate moors, heather ablur beneath the pounding horses' hoofs. Glen to glen we skirt past villages all the night, ever alert for the lurking enemy.

As the first light of day reddens the snow-covered peaks, we sprint toward the Cairngorm Mountains. It would not be long now. Over these hills lie safety and our Queen. Suddenly from all sides they are upon us, claymores slashing. Outnumbered three to one, Dave and I are cornered against the banks of the swirling River Spey. We dismount and square off opposite the six Orangemen of the Earl. By twos they come at us. The air fills with the hollow ring of clashing metal and the flashing glint of steel. Our swords find their mark through kilt and armored waistcoat. One by one they fall. They are no match for us.

Now all but one of them is dropped, and he is by far the vilest of the lot. Like some immense oaken tree trunk he towers over us, staring out of his wart-covered face with beady red eyes stuck one next to the other. From head to foot his body is covered by a mat of coarse brown hair, making him appear more beast than man. With a bloodcurdling scream the ogre charges at Dave and me, sweeping his great broadsword in a mighty arc about our throats. Momentarily we fall back, and then we lunge out at him on the attack, swords meeting in a shower of sparks. Time and again we try for the advantage, but he rebuffs us. What kind of creature is this? Together Dave and I are barely a match for him, so quick, so strong, so agile.

Now with a grunt he pounces upon me, slicing a great downward blow toward my head. I block it but am thrown to the ground, claymore shattered in half. Defenseless, I lie stunned upon the riverbank. The ogre moves in for the kill. Towering over my side, he raises his sword high above his head, then hesitates, emitting a grating howl. Trembling with fear, I close my eyes, awaiting death's blow. I feel the *whoosh* of the sailing blade as its sinister shadow flickers over my eyes in the morning sun. I black out. It is hours before I come to. I open my eyes to the setting sun. I am unwounded save for a large welt on my forehead. Beside me, lying stiff upon the moor, is the bloody severed arm of the ogre, broadsword still clenched in its fist. The monster is nowhere to be seen, nor is Dave. I mount my steed to look for him. It is in the village of Rannock that I hear the news. Queen Mary has fallen and fled to England for her life. I head westward away from my fallen Queen in search of Dave.

VIII

Is it just a fantasy?
To seek a face
So pure
So free

Anticipation drives us from the warmth of our sleeping bags in the predawn hours of Friday the thirteenth, and we are soon plodding along under cold, clear skies across the last of the open moors toward the Breach Wall. The ground is frozen. Above, the inky sky is filled with night lights—the Southern Cross, Volans, Corena, Centauris, Southern Hemisphere stars and constellations I have read about but not seen. By the time the stars have faded, we reach the cliffs of the Window Buttress, a shattered stairway of large, steep ledges, its top pierced by a two-hundred-foot hole. The land of the living, with its tuft grasses, mosses, and alpine flowers, its world of smells, is left behind now. We enter the barren realm of rock and ice, the lava deserts of Kilimanjaro. Here only the hardiest of lichens can be found tucked away in rock crevices.

After two hours of clambering up the black rock of the lower buttress, we reach the snout of the Heim Glacier. The buttress continues upward straight ahead toward the Breach Wall, and the ice of the glacier parallels it off to the right before eventually arcing back over to the peak of the buttress. From this point forward our route leaves behind the rock and will be entirely on ice and snow. Just as water always seeks the path of least resistance, so, too, here does the ice, its frozen counterpart, offering a direct line up the Wall. Shorts and shirtsleeves are abandoned for fleece underwear and Gore-Tex climbing suits. Ice axes and crampons are strapped on; then we set off soloing the lower reaches of the Heim, a slick slide of ice whose angle, slightly steeper than the roof of an Alpine chalet, presents little difficulty. It is a joy to be climbing once again. Harley and I ascend side by side, yards apart, saying little, totally absorbed by the magical trance of our icy dance up the glacier. We rapidly gain height; far below us we can see the mounding cumulus clouds ascending the mountain valleys like some raging torrent defying gravity. By 10 A.M. the mists overtake and swarm upon us. In all likelihood this is to be the prevailing weather pattern on Kili, and one can expect only three clear hours daily for climbing. If it were just a problem with visibility, we could proceed by meticulous route-finding, charting a course by the prominent landmarks we saw earlier on the face. However, after thirty minutes of climbing, I notice that the firm, compact snow-ice surface has become nothing more than a veneer over a rotten, internally honeycombed mass. When the mist envelops this surface, instead of preserving its integrity and protecting it from the sun, it causes it to turn into mush allowing little security. This makes for easy but insecure and unreliable cramponing. When I see that Harley's climbing technique shows no reflection of the changed conditions, I break the morning's spell of tranquility with a caution. "Harley, this stuff is unstable underneath. We've got to be careful on it."

He shouts back, "Whaddya talking about?" He digs his boot tip into the slush and balances on it, holding hands and the other foot in the air. "This snow's a hundred percent safe. Just look at the good time we're making. Don't get so hyped up."

I take the lead, making a rightward rising traverse, soon arriving at the edge of a dirty shallow trough the width of a dual-lane highway and about the same color. I trace its line upward until it disappears into the clouds. Debris chutes like this catch falling particles of ice, rock, or snow and funnel them down the mountainside, often at tremendous speeds. Our proposed route lies directly across the chute. I stop and listen for the sound of anything moving up above and, hearing nothing, dart across the trench. Once on the other side, I look back at Harley's passage. He does not even hesitate at the chute's edge; showing no recognition of the trough's existence, he saunters across. In the middle, he stops to snap a photo. When he arrives by my side without mishap, he speaks first.

"What the hell has gotten into you, Rob? Why were you running like a scared rabbit?"

"Do you realize you could have been killed twice over in the amount of time you took crossing that chute?"

"What chute? You mean that little streak of gray ice? You're crazy. I don't know what kinda head problems you're having, but I'll tell you this: you can't move around like that at this altitude; you'll never make it."

He passes me by and heads toward the final steep ice cliffs leading up to the Silver Saddle, the broad col of ice near the top of the Window Buttress. The angle of the slope ahead rises sharply, approaching 70 degrees in places. Though the snow conditions continue to deteriorate, Harley carries on with his kick-step routine, unperplexed. Only when he tries to surmount a particularly nasty bulge of snow and suddenly both feet cut loose, leaving him dangling by one arm from his ice ax, do I see concern for the first time on his face. He calls for the rope. We tie on and I suggest he take the lead, knowing he would want to anyway, but also thinking that the snow is so bad now that either of us could easily fall. In such conditions the responsibility for the climbing team is on the second man. Despite the impossibility of getting a sure anchor, he must be able to hold any slip, fall, or slide.

Blindly we grope our way through the final maze of ice cliffs. I sense at any moment that the entire wall of slush around us will just slide free, curling down like some enormous breaking tidal wave. When I offer a suggestion as to route or a warning of danger to Harley, he disdainfully replies that I am much too worrisome and paranoid to be in the mountains. After being reminded of this several times, I begin to wonder if this may be true and my years of avalanche experience for naught.

By noon the last of the glacier and lower headwall is beneath us. With the visibility now down to twenty feet, we set about trying to find the small rocky peak of the Window Buttress. After some minutes of aimless wandering I locate the rock tower and beneath it two small ledges, likely-looking bivouac sites. Unsatisfied with my find, "not big enough for rats' asses," Harley goes off in search of a proper place to spend the night. Shortly he returns luckless and reluctantly settles for the remaining lower ledge. Six inches to our left, the security of our perch abruptly ends with a two-thousand-foot drop down onto the lower wall we have climbed past this morning. Not that we have any views of it in this pea-soup fog, but this is no ground for sleepwalkers. We are settled in not twenty minutes when the first of many large avalanches begins breaking away and rumbling down the ice fall and trough we passed only an hour earlier. Though we are protected and safe on our rock peak, there is something frighteningly awesome about the power of nature's fury being unleashed so close. Lying in my bivy sack, all hell breaking loose around us, I have second thoughts about Harley's comprehension of the present conditions on the mountain and his grasp of the consequences that might befall us. His carefree, nonchalant attitude makes me wonder if he realizes the severity of our position. Alpine climbing entails more than the acquisition of technical skills to overcome a series of isolated difficulties during an ascent. It demands the ability to assess the overall situation en route, make the proper judgment, and act accordingly. Alpine climbing demands almost a sixth sense that allows one to perceive the slightest changes and adapt oneself simultaneously to them. In the present circumstances, I realize, one of the changes I must somehow adapt to is the attitude of Harley Warner.

*   *   *

The morning of Saturday, January 14, once again comes in clear, cold, and black. As we brew up, still in our pits, there looms out of the darkness above us the main Breach Icefield, and there at the top of it, glinting through the blackness, that incredible needle of an icicle. We thaw frozen boots over the small gas jet of our stove and are away from our bivouac by seven, slowly soloing a rising leftward traverse onto the steep field of ice. Seventeen thousand feet below, clouds blanket the plains of Africa. The sun rises a deep maroon, turning these clouds into a boiling caldron of blood. For all his boasting yesterday, Harley is going slowly today, lagging behind hundreds of feet until I stop and allow him to close the distance before moving on. I wonder if his barb about my being a frightened rabbit was really a cover for his own lack of conditioning.

As the angle increases drastically, we rope up but continue to move together, the leader driving in ice screws for protection and the second removing them as he climbs past. The type of ice here is changed from the former carvable, frothy, opaque-white medium whose consistency fluctuated widely with the changing temperature. Now the face is pure water ice, shiny, brittle, deep blue. It takes many blows of the ice ax just to make a nick in the dense surface, almost like hitting a steel girder with a hammer. From the gouged, streaked, and pitted appearance of the icefield surface—evidence of the pellets and blocks of lava and ice that drop from the summit in the heat of day—it is apparent that at times this would be a very dangerous place to be. As we press on and the equatorial sun rises higher and higher, the day becomes unusually warm. By the time we reach the base of the icicle, it is just before noon, and great spouts of water are pouring off Kili's summit crater and streaming down into space.

I gaze up at the dripping, rotting cylinder of ice stretching three hundred vertical feet to the top of the Breach Wall. My first reaction is awe, then recoil. It is obvious that this Breach Icicle just isn't in "knick" at present, and, besides, to go on it now in the heat of the afternoon would be suicidal. This I say to Harley and add that I feel we ought to bivouac and attempt it around three or four the next morning. To be honest, even after waiting for a night's hard freeze I give us only a fifty-fifty chance for success. Its condition is too deteriorated, having no solid consistency. Harley disagrees, violently so, insisting that under no circumstances is he going to sit around for sixteen hours and wait now that we are so close to success, adding that it would give us a greater chance tomorrow should we fail to knock it off today.

Knocking heads was nothing new on this trip, but this one disagreement is direct and total. We repeat our arguments at irreconcilable loggerheads. Stalemate. Soundless minutes pass with us standing there at over eighteen thousand feet beneath the icicle. Then Harley takes a different tack. "Ya know, Rob, this trip has shown me a different side of you, one I have no respect for. You used to be a great ice climber, but you've lost your nerve. You don't belong in this occupation." He pours forth a confusing mixture of flattery and abuse, his tirade overwhelming me like an avalanche itself. His self-assurance suddenly is as intimidating as a force of nature. In the end I find myself reluctantly conceding to give the icicle a try without even realizing I'm saying it or why I'm saying it. Man often tends to justify his questionable actions with inane or nebulous rationalizations. Today I am no exception. Although I feel that under present conditions a fall is a very real possibility, I justify my course of action by thinking I will be extracautious. I will overprotect on the icicle with closely spaced ice screws, thus remaining in control even if a fall does occur.

Without a word between us I begin climbing. The ice on the icicle is the worst I have ever encountered. To a depth of three feet, the surface is composed of fragile latticed striations of rotted ice crystals which collapse at the slightest touch. For each tenuous placement of the ax, this sugary surface must first be cleared away. It is a strenuous task at this altitude, and I quickly find myself fully extended just trying to stay in contact with the decomposed vertical sludge. At a point approximately twenty feet above Harley, I clear away the outer layer and place an ice screw deep within the good bed ice of the icicle, then traverse past it until it is within a few feet of my right boot. The ice degenerates here from bad to worse; no longer will it hold my ice axes. I lock my gloved palms around a projecting pedestal of ice resembling a giant head of cauliflower. Above, off to my extreme left, the ice appears slightly better, more consolidated, and I decide to head for it. Clutching the knobbed ice mass to my chest, delicately I move up, then push off it. I stretch my limit across to reach the better ice and drive my ax home into it. In the midst of this maneuver the pedestal snaps off upon me. I fly back into space. I'm falling! I lunge for the secured climbing rope beside me.

Dazed, I slowly revolve, hanging horizontally in the air, staring up at Harley. By rights, with protection so close at hand, it should have been no more than a very short, three- or four-foot, fall. Did the screw come out? Suddenly I am aware of pain in my left foot. I stare down in horror. Instead of seeing the top of my red-and-blue Supergator, I see only the twelve points of my Chouinard crampons and my boot sole. The arch of my foot is wrenched around, touching my inner calf. I look to Harley. "I can't believe it! My ankle's broken."

"Are you sure?"

"Of course I'm sure!"

"Isn't that great!" says Harley, smiling. "Just like every other damn thing on this trip."

"How could I have been so stupid to go on this thing in the first place!" Looking up, I see that the ice screw held. "What happened?"

"I guess I let the rope slip."

Suddenly it all makes sense. My fall was sudden, catching Harley unaware. I smashed feet first into a sloping ledge at the base of the icicle before Harley regained control of the rope.

What now? Harley suggests we keep going up the icicle with

him leading. "After I get up, you can follow behind on a top rope with Jumar clamps. I can leave you on the top, then go over the summit and down the tourist route for help."

"No. No matter what you do, I am going nowhere but down."

In a span of seconds, Harley's look changes from disbelief to disappointment to annoyance, yet he remains silent. My reasoning for descent is simple. The icicle is unclimbable by anyone, at least today. Also, the possibility of shock increases with altitude. Last and most important, Kilimanjaro has one of the broadest summit plateaus in the world. I have heard of numerous examples of people lost for days, even permanently, in the mists on Kili's great snow dome. With the present weather conditions, this is more a probability. I force the issue for descent. For once, Harley concedes.

From our vantage point, protected by the angle of the jutting wall above us and clinging to 70-degree-angle ice at the base of the final Breach Buttress, we can see an incredible amount of debris falling onto the icefield below. An attempt to retreat across it now would mean certain death. Even Harley's eyes register the danger. Although I am anxious to get down as quickly as possible, there is no choice but to stop and bivy. I direct Harley to lead off rightward to a small ledge we discovered earlier this morning. It is several hundred feet away, safely tucked beneath overhanging rock cliffs, offering excellent protection from falling debris. Harley traverses toward the ledge and I follow, a strenuous procedure because of my useless left leg and further complicated by the loss of two ice axes in the fall. Surprisingly, however, I find, because of the steep pitch, I can manipulate quite well and make good time by using my left knee as a substitute foot, cutting a small step for it while balancing on the front points of my right crampon. All the while I ponder the extent of my injury, praying that the break not be compound.

As soon as I arrive in the hollow, I set about gingerly undoing my gaiter and loosening my bootlaces. I must slacken them sufficiently to allow me to probe the grossly distorted area on the outside of my ankle. Yet under no circumstances do I want to remove my boot, as I will never be able to get it back on. I almost retch when my searching fingers locate the greasy protruding end of my fibula. I quickly yank out my blood-covered hand and stare in disbelief as drop by drop it stains the ice beside me.

Suddenly the severity and hopelessness of the situation strikes me. I realize that this time I shall die. There is no escape. We are now at over eighteen thousand feet, nearly seventy-five miles from the nearest medical help. Long before I can hope to reach any proper assistance, gangrene and infection will take their toll. The staccato pounding of my heart fills my head, ears ringing, eyes dazzled white; it is all I can do to fight off the insidious sweeping haze of shock and prevent it from overcoming me. I look to Harley, but he is down at the opposite end of our ledge. Head craned out over the icefield, he clicks shot after shot of the aerial bombardment unfolding below.

As bad as things are, I see the choices quite clearly. Shock is immediate death; in fighting I have at least a chance. I lean against the uneven coarse brown pumice, searching my brain for some hint or clue I may have forgotten that will help me decide what to do. The options are obvious: either leave it and splint it where it lies and have no foot by morning, just a dead, black mass waiting to be cut off; or reduce the fracture and chance knicking an artery with the fibula and die in a pool of my own blood in a matter of minutes. I opt for reduction and call Harley over to lend a hand. "It's a compound fracture, Harley; it's open and bleeding."

"Oh," he says distractedly, "that bad, huh?"

"It's risky, but I'm going to try and get the bones back in line. I want you to grab hold of my left boot and keep it straight and level. I'll do the rest."

I align upper torso, thigh, knee, and calf in direct line with my foot and pull against Harley's resistance on my boot. Again and again. After some minutes of painful, tense effort, the fibula pop back into place. I promptly splint it under tension with an ice-hammer shaft, some crampon parts, and the hip belt from my pack. The pain subsides. I settle into my sleeping bag for the long night ahead.

Before he falls asleep, Harley says to me, "Rob, do you believe in God?"

I nod weakly.

"Well, I don't personally," he continues, "but if you do, I'd start praying. You're going to need all the help you can get for this one."

The morning of January 15, we are awake before the dawn. It has been a fitful night for me, still I feel no further deterioration since yesterday's trauma. Harley tends to a breakfast of minestrone soup and polenta while I prepare my leg for the day's rigors. I take a twenty-foot length of one-inch nylon webbing and wrap it securely around the boot and lower calf of my injured leg in overlapping circles. Makeshift cradle complete, I hoist the leg up behind me until boot back touches my buttocks, and secure it in place by strapping it to my climbing harness waistbelt. Ten minutes later and we are away from the bivouac, retracing our steps across the broad Breach Icefield still cloaked in shadow. Speed is everything today, both for my leg's survival and for our safe passage across the range of falling debris. Already beneath us the Window Buttress is aglow in the sun's first light. The descent is laborious. I find that the harness I have rigged creates a constant tension which not only eases the pain in my ankle but also gives me added stability. I am able to make good progress considering the severity of my incapacity. Rope length after rope length we descend, leaving one screw as an anchor for each rappel, Harley always going first, sliding down the rope, at the end securing it and pulling tension to facilitate my diagonal passage across. I experiment with a number of different trial maneuvers such as hopping, sliding feet first, and kneeling, before finding that head-first, downhill lying on my right side is the fastest and least painful method for getting down. Try as I may, it is not fast enough.

Peeved at my slowness, Harley barks directions, "Come on, get a move on. Don't cross those goddamn ropes or I'll send you back to untangle them." His involvement with me is strictly business, the business of getting down the face. At this he is most efficient, yet there is none of the human support or compassion I need in addition. The only bond between us is the fifty meters of climbing rope.

Once we are three-quarters across the icefield, safely out of harm's way, I yell to him, "I've got to stop and rest a few minutes. I've got no strength left in my arms. If you make the route straight down now it will be much easier for me."

He screams back, "You cut that chickenshit whining right now or I'm gonna cut the goddamn rope and leave you up here."

Silently I continue down. The anger in his tone makes me suspect that such an action by him is not beyond possibility.

After several final pendulums, we reach the right-hand edge of the icefield. I am utterly exhausted, yet we have five hundred feet of lower-angled slope to descend before reaching the Window Buttress. I start down on hands and knees. It is remarkable what extreme stress can do for perspective. Only yesterday I climbed this very slope with the security of two ice axes and crampons, taking much care with my movements. Now I crawl down on my belly, unroped, unprotected, uncaring for anything except to reach the bottom. The last remnants of my strength ebb away as I collapse onto the rocks of the Window Buttress peak.

I look down and see that blood has saturated the outside of my gaiter. So intense has my concentration been that I have not even noticed the blood working its way through the three pairs of socks, the boot, and the gaiter. It stains the snow beneath a pastel pink. Eager as I am to get to the base of the Wall today despite the soupy mist that has again engulfed us, I accede to Harley's desire to bivouac when I hear the sporadic roar and rumble of the headwall ice cliffs beneath us, breaking off and strafing the lower face.

The sun is already up and shining brightly on the Silver Saddle on the morning of January 16 as I slowly shake off the peaceful sleep that provided so much comfort, protection, and escape. Full reality returns to my dull and deadened senses over a brew of warm fruit tea, the last of our food. As I unzip my sleeping bag, I catch a faint but distinct odor, similar to that of an overripe, rotting pear. I call Harley over, but the smell lasts but a second, vanishing in the fresh morning air.

"There's nothing there, Rob, only the smell of your boot leather. You're letting your imagination run wild again." He turns to prepare for the descent. Am I imagining things?

Because of the multiple ice cliffs that comprise the Heim, reversing this section proves by far the most dangerous and difficult. This is aggravated by the fact that we no longer have any ice screws left and have to rely solely on ax-boot belays for security. We creep downward as carefully as possible. His lowering me down over the overhanging serac walls causes much jolting to my ankle, which again is spilling fresh blood from my boot back. I, in turn, must belay him down. Painstakingly we negotiate pitch after pitch of the steep ice and unconsolidated snow. It is only after the mist swallows us up and for the first time it begins snowing that we finally arrive at the snout of the ice. In the heavy fog we are there several minutes before we even realize our location.

After so many days of verticality, it is wonderful to be on ground that you can't fall off. But it also becomes immediately obvious that with the loss of steepness comes also the loss of my mobility. My controlled lowering and sliding gives way to groveling only a few meters at a time on my chest. There is little choice now in the manner of descent. I can't walk, and Harley can't carry me very far. He must leave and go for help. The Horombo Hut, which has a radio, is approximately six hours' hike to the east. So we agree that Harley will go there.

But first we must get off this ice. I toss away my remaining crampon and ice hammer, along with the remainder of my superfluous climbing equipment. The additional weight will only be a burden. Then I sling my arms over Harley's shoulders, and he carries me on his back down from the glacier's edge across the sandy moraine to a ledge about five hundred feet below, on the lee side of several large boulders. The arguing, the ill-feeling between us up on the Wall, seems to have dissipated.

I settle back into my sleeping bag and bivy sack while Harley readies himself for departure. I watch with amusement as he neatly packs away all his equipment, including climbing gear, ice axes, crampons, slings, and carabiners into his sack. I cannot help wondering why he would want to carry all that extra weight while running for help. Once again we rehash plans about Harley's going to the Horombo Hut.

"OK, Rob, I'm off—be back late tonight or very early tomorrow morning with the rescue party. I am going to run all the way, so there is a chance I might be too tired to return. But I'll make sure they have the three things you want: antibiotics, antiseptic, and painkiller. Take it easy—rest, the worst is over now. I'm gonna take care of everything, so don't worry. I'll make all the arrangements with the doctors, the hospital, and for surgery. We've made it this far; we'll make it all the way."

It is midmorning as I stare down across mottled white moraines for a long while and think to myself, I am alive! I've made it. I watch Harley's blue-clad figure slowly vanish below into a curtain of heavy falling snow. What a picture this would make. I grab my sack beside me and quickly rifle through it for the thirty-five-millimeter Olympus. It's not here. I look up. Harley is gone as well.

IX

Hey you!
Have you come to comfort me
Or take me for your own?

There is nothing to do now but wait. In only hours Harley will return. I lie back. Relax, get some rest. I cannot. My body tingles with excitement. Tears of joy moisten my eyes. It is more than anxious anticipation of Harley's imminent return with help. It's actually over! "I have made it," I shout to the snow-filled heavens. That day at the icicle, high up on the Breach Wall, God rose before me and presented to me a challenge. Into my hands He entrusted for a time the supreme power of choice—life or death. He did not abandon me in my trial. I sensed His nearness. But the choice was mine and mine alone to make. Whatever path I struck for, I felt He would accede to my decision. He would be there, helping me on my way. But what direction? It rested in my hands. I chose life and hence the challenges that accompany life. The descent. The days of struggle. The gnawing uncertainties. Would I be strong enough? Could I keep this leg? Would it all be for nothing in the end? The fight for survival was not so much a quest for life as an ever constant vigil against Death. Time and again I saw the sweep of his black, sinister shadow run across my eyes. I felt his icy, foul breath upon my shoulder. During our retreat from the wall he stalked my every move, waiting, watchful for my weakening.

I feel as if I have shaken this relentless escort. He is gone. For the first time I relax my guard. I am safe. From within there glows a satisfaction with myself and a gratefulness to God for having bestowed upon me the will and strength to survive. During my first day's vigil I begin experiencing firsthand all sorts of astonishing feelings and emotions—things I never imagined an individual would undergo when caught out alone in a desperate situation. Contrary to my preconceived notions of how I would react in such a situation, I am not filled with an ever increasing dread and despair by the hour. Instead a deep, soothing tranquility sweeps over me. I calmly sink into a self-induced trance and find myself able to resolve heretofore incomprehensible and insoluble inner conflicts with a snap. It is not so much a process of self-examination as of self-contemplation, of being suddenly able to view oneself from the vantage point of a third person. Happy, reassured, I soon drift off to that secret enchanted kingdom which all men for a time may inhabit without worry or concern. Sleep.

I start awake. Momentarily I am disoriented by the blackness of night. It shrouds all features. Where am I? Reality returns: Africa, the fall, Kilimanjaro, Harley, the Breach Wall, waiting, waiting for help. Glancing down at my watch, I press the light button. The window displays a crisp black 12:38. More than twelve hours have passed since Harley left for help. Is that what awoke me—calls from the rescue party returning with Harley? I lean forward, pulling off my woolen balaclava, and look into the night. I try to pierce the darkness for a sign: bouncing yellow pinpricks of light, telltale signs of rescue fast approaching. How I yearn for them to be there. Holding back a breath, I listen, receptive to any sound the world may offer. Nothing. I am immersed in a realm of silence, vacant of noise. Its roar is deafening. I speak aloud to myself for assurance that I have not gone deaf. I am sealed in this maddening vacuum like the deep-sea diver in the depths of the ocean. I see. I touch. The world surrounds me, yet I hear not. Within stirs the slightest twinge of uneasiness. For the first time I sense how truly alone I am in this alien, barren desert of rock and snow. Not just alone, something more. Immobile, defenseless, I am helplessly alone. Vulnerable. Shivering, I snuggle back deep into my sleeping bag, suddenly feeling exposed. To whom? And threatened. By what? I try to reason, yet my urgency grows. When I was small, I dreaded the fall of night, that eventual hour bidding me to sleep, alone, immersed in a darkness that took my sight and shuttered away all colors of life. Upon my bed, my isle of safety, I had only the feeble square borders of the mattress as protection against the turbulent sea of blackness just beyond—and all the horrors of the imagination that hid there. Now, after all these years, once more I am this child. I share his fear. Unwittingly there creeps into my mind the inevitable thought, What if no one comes . . . at all? It is only for a second, and then I force Harley's words to the front of my mind, "Be back late tonight or first light tomorrow." Don't worry, he'll be here, I reassure myself, relaxing back into sleep.

The amber light of dawn gradually filters through the yellow cocoon of my bivouac sack, awakening me. Great! It's sunny. Nothing lifts the spirit more than a bright sunny morning. It says to the world, "Don't worry, all is well. It's a new shining day full of promise and hope." The good weather will also make for that much swifter and easier rescue. I slit the Velcro on the protective hood of my Gore-Tex bivy and peer out to disappointment and skies still full of falling snow. The gold-tinted fabric of the bivy sack has only created the illusion of a sunrise, of warmth and hope. Reality, instead, is marked in infinite shades of gray and white, from sky to snow, from hazy mottled landscape to the void below. It is a realm of neutral tones. Where I lay upon bare moraine yesterday, now the snow is mounded up to the depth of more than a foot over me. And it continues accumulating rapidly. One consolation is that I didn't give in to Harley when he wanted to push on to the summit. I could well visualize our plight had we made it to the top: lost for days in this whiteout at nearly twenty thousand feet up on the fifty square miles of summit slopes, not knowing which way was up, which way down, wandering aimlessly in circles till we both dropped dead from exhaustion amidst the rumbling airborne avalanches that would now be strafing the breadth of the Breach, launching a million tons of snow. We were at least alive today because of my decision. It was the right one, and, more important, I had stuck by it.

I check my watch: 8:05. I am surprised it is so late, yet so murky still. The drab skies cloud any indication of the passage of time. Day or night, morning or afternoon, each is differentiated from the other by only gradual increments in a variety of bland shades, charcoal to ashen, then back again. Well, they must be here any time now. I search the endless white moraines, which fade below into snowy haze, for black specks of movement. So irrepressible is my anticipation that, seeing not a trace, I am genuinely surprised. Again I cock an ear, keen for any sound. Nothing. Save for the softly wailing wind, the falling snow. In this realm of silence, even the sound of snowflakes seems thunderous. I listen to the *tush, tush, tush* as each comes crashing down to destruction upon the ground. In times past I would never have given them a second's notice. Now they are sensory comfort, God-sent soothing music to my ears.

It is strange. God is so much in my thoughts these days. More than just present circumstances bring Him to mind—the hard times, a fear of dying, remorse over past actions. There is something special of Him here—on the flanks of this mountain. His presence hangs in the air like the smell of burning incense. I cannot smell it, but almost. I can almost touch it, almost taste it. Yet my eyes see nothing, my ears hear nothing. It is a feeling whose origin lies beyond the usual boundaries of flesh and spirit. I feel His presence as if I were immersed in His being. I sense His presence as you can sense the presence of a friend in his house when you're in different rooms even though he's not visible to you and not talking to you—just there. I have never had such a feeling before in any church or cathedral. Not in any place of man. Was this what the ancient Masai warriors sensed when they called this mountain's western summit Ngaje Ngai, the House of God? Was this what the leopard, frozen in his quest, was seeking at this altitude? I have never been much of a prayer-sayer, couldn't bring myself to spout verse to empty space or some plastic statuette. Nothing changes now. There is no need for prayers. The lines of communication between God and me transcend words, perhaps even thoughts, reaching to the soul itself. While I am a solitary man upon this mountain, I am not alone. I am watched over. I am close to home. I sense it so strongly, it is almost frightening.

How is it faring now? I recall the past days: the descent, the trauma to it, so much jerking, so many blows, the blood spilling out the boot back. How much worse is the foot for this abuse? Will it be a deciding factor on whether I keep my leg or lose it? I tell myself I had no choice, it was life or death, I did the best I could, I've made it this far, I am going to live. Only God can decide now whether it will be with my leg. I must leave my fate in His hands. This is not so easy to accept, not for me, considering my life of climbing, a life of self-sufficiency, of self-reliance. We have all invoked the Lord's name in secret prayer at times in those tough spots, an accident, financial ruin, marital problems, only to promptly forget Him when all is resolved by ourselves or the doctor or the judge. No one is going to resolve this for me. I am beyond human controls. I have no options. It is for keeps, and what is at stake is not an idle whim or desire for money or success. It is a leg, my leg. A leg whose future now rests with a higher being. What if He deems I shall lose it? What would I do?

Never to run, never to climb again. No mountains, ever. Would I even want to live without it? The question rattles disturbingly around in my head. Worst of all is the not knowing. What state is it in now? Blindly my fingers search within the tight confines of my sleeping bag, probing over the bulging, splinted area covering my ankle. As I move, stabs of pain shoot through my body. The pain was so much lessened while I lay still, I have forgotten its intensity and dropped my guard. It takes only a tensing of the muscles now to release its fury once again. It is a jolt like being hit with 120 volts of current, only there is no one to turn off the power. Or is there? High up on the Wall, on the descent, the pain was intolerable. More than I could stand, I thought. I prayed for the relief of death. Unlike electricity, severe pain, I soon found out, would not kill me. As well, I realized, trying to ignore it did not make it decrease or go away. Like a dog chasing a running coward, pain pursues all the more those who try to run away from it. It was necessary to face the pain head on and come to terms with it. That meant feeling its intensity, measuring it, and assenting to its presence, its control, and its duration. Once the pain was thus sounded and accepted, its ferocity diminished. Not that it ever disappeared completely, but I discovered that, within, man has the capacity for containing pain. I realized that his tolerance is almost limitless if the power of his mind is great enough.

I lean forward to sniff the air inside my sleeping bag. Eyes closed, once, twice, three times I draw in long deep breaths, channeling every ounce of energy to my nose, my sense of smell, alert to any trace of that horrid, foul scent. "Nothing," I exhale with relief. To be extra certain, again I inhale. It smells of stale sweat, damp wool, and soggy down. And, oddly enough, of simmering chicken soup, the kind my grandmother makes with escarole and beaten egg. Perhaps she was making some now. My mind jumps at the opportunity of returning home. Suddenly she is there before my mind's eye, small, gray, almost mouselike, huddled over her old cook stove. Lovingly she strokes the steaming, bubbling broth with her wooden ladle. She looks up at me—vanishing. What have I been thinking about? Searching for my lost train of thought, mindlessly I glance down at my timepiece: 9:47. I remember. Of course, my leg. There's no odor! Perhaps it really isn't so serious as I suspected. Again I check the time, 9:50, then catch myself. It has been only minutes since I last looked. In this present existence of mine, all encompassed by waiting, time and its passage have taken on a strange new importance. Like each breath, like each beat of the heart, checking the time becomes not so much an obsession as an involuntary compulsion. I seek it more out of nervous necessity than want of the hour. Whatever the case, it passes all too slowly.

Where can Harley be? It is almost midmorning. He said, "First light." Sudden alarm catches me off guard. Quickly I bridle it with reasoning. Even under perfect conditions in the mountains, an individual normally has to be given at least twenty-four hours leeway. There are too many unknown factors, decisive factors, to be considered. With Harley, now, I know full well that any number of unforeseen reasons could be delaying his return. This storm, for one. Deep snow upon the trail would make for rough going, and perhaps it was longer than we thought to Horombo, and returning, that long uphill slog in the snow. He would be tired, maybe a lot slower than he anticipated. Any and all of them are too plausible. In the end, more than one of them likely would be the cause of Harley's delay in getting back. For the present I hearten myself not to worry. Certainly he will come any time now. Anyway I am comfortable and in no immediate grave danger. It is three days since the accident, and I appear to be getting no worse. I can still feel my toes when I wiggle them, and there's no odor—if there really ever was any odor. A few hours more or less will probably make little difference in the long run.

But will it? Uncertainty returns and with it the vision of a wooden stump just below my knee. It is vivid. I scan the polished mahogany surface, tracing the dark arched grain ringing the wood, cold senseless wood replacing warm vibrant flesh. Is this what lies in store for me? I drive the scene from my mind. Already God has given me life. I must keep my faith. I'm in good shape now. I recall the old medical advice, "Fluid helps fight infection," and decide to make some tea. I've had nothing since Harley's departure yesterday. I scoop a panful of snow and place it upon the small butane gas stove beside me. I open the gas jet and light the stove. A ring of yellow, then blue flame bursts forth. The steady high resonant chugging of the burner—that familiar sizzle of melting snow against the aluminum pan bottom—is a welcome sound. Soon there will be more warm water than I can drink. I cup my hands around the cooker to catch the escaping heat. In less than a minute the stove begins wildly sputtering, alternating balls of flashing green fire with meager violet flickering flames. I hasten to readjust it, to catch it before it goes out, but it flutters and dies. Try as I may with the remaining matches, it will not relight. I check the cartridge. Empty. Of all the things I can do without, water is not one. Without it I cannot survive. I grasp the useless stove and hurl it into the mist. Downward it rattles hollowly, out of sight, as I stare into space, wondering what to do now.

Then I see him—or it—for the first time. My pulse quickens. It must be one of the rescue party. A figure crouches not fifty yards from me. "Hello over there! Helloooo!" I yell. No response. I believe that my eyes must be playing tricks on me, taking some lump of rock to be a man. I blink several times as if to clear my eyes; yet there he sits atop a large boulder, clearly distinct from the rock below him. Again I yell, "Hello! Over here! Have you come to save me?" Again no response. Now I don't believe my eyes at all—it's not really there—just hallucination, a mirage. But he does not fade away. Try as I may to close my eyes and wish him gone, every time I open them he remains. He will not go. My joy, long since modified to weariness of this game, changes now to fear. "Who are you? What do you want? Answer me!" To no effect. In my frustration I begin lobbing fist-size chunks of pumice at him in an attempt to elicit some response, if only to stir him from his perch. Across the void between us I launch projectile after projectile, trying to bean him, with no success. All my throws fall far short, or are they too long? Several times stones are in perfect line for a direct score, only to pass by him or through him unimpeded. None of them ever hits him. I cannot understand. Clearly I make out his form, yet never can I distinguish exact features through the snowy haze. So taut are the general lines of his body, he appears devoid of clothing, like a dancer in a leotard. Chin in hand, elbow on knee, this drab, gray being certainly looks human but somehow is not. The heavily falling snow continues to mound upon me, but not a single flake lies upon his countenance. Ever downward drift the multitudes of lacy crystals accumulating deeply on the ground around him, yet somehow he escapes their icy embrace. How can this be? Hour upon hour this companion watcher, as I call him, peers out at me through the curtain of snow. And I at him, full of puzzlement. Serenely he surveys me, keeping me company in my long watch, yet, as if oblivious to me, never does he acknowledge my calls or make any movement toward me.

Man's natural penchant for intelligent order forces him to fit all things, be they spiritual, material, or other, into neat proper places within his psyche, if only for perspective. A thing may not be fully understood, yet at least it can be allotted an appropriate niche in the mind, classified as "like this" or "similar to that." With this companion watcher I am lost. My mind does not know what to do with him. Each change of thought brings to me another swell and ebb in a sea of varying emotions. There is fear: he is like the jackal who, with that sixth sense for death, sits and waits. It is only a matter of time until I am his. Then hope: he is a guardian, watching over me, my protector. Then loathing: he is a messenger of Satan come to claim his due for eternity. Then joy: he is a benevolent sign reinforcing my spirit not to give up—rescue will soon be here. Even despair: he is but an emissary from the netherworld to lead me on my final journey. In the deepening gray of afternoon I turn away from him, lying back to rest, troubled, wondering. What can this creature want? If only I could walk, go over, talk to it. Why is he here now? In deep thought I dwell for a time till my ears prick at a faint new sound. So familiar, *drip, drip, drip*, like the soft murmur of a leaky faucet. Water. Where can it be coming from? I follow my ears, trying to locate its source. Ever faster the steady dripping grows. At last I find it beneath the downhill side of my bivouac sack. Water. The droplets dribble from my side onto a small patch of bare ground, the only bare ground beneath me. Of course! The heat of my body has risen upward to the snow on top of me and melted it into water. So simple. Suddenly it is clear to me, I have the resources to produce as much water as I want. I shrug off the great bank of snow that covers me and form a shallow indented trough in the surface of my bivouac sack between my legs. Next I fill this shallow basin with a small quantity of snow. In only minutes it melts from my body heat into water. I drain this off into the cooking pot, place more snow in the trough, repeat the procedure. Within the hour my liter cooking pot is full. Now I may drink my fill. A minute's frantic gulping, and the pot is empty, yet I am satisfied. I feel refreshed, vibrant, full of life once more. As I continue with the snow-melting procedure to prepare water for later, my spirit glows anew. Perhaps this companion watcher is more guardian than I realized. After all, my discovery of water came just after his appearance. A good omen, and he continues to wait with me.

Everything is going to be fine. Harley will probably even bring a doctor along. With the antibiotics they will bring I am assured of keeping my leg alive. And by tomorrow afternoon I will be at a hospital safe, secure, ensconced in its warm white sterility under the watchful eyes of doctors and nurses. They will help me, take my struggle as their own. I will need to fight no more. Strange how it all seems so appealing now, a hospital, usually the place I avoided at any cost. At home the mere sight of Emerson Hospital's ivy-clad walls, up the short winding drive, brought on the sweaty flush of nervous apprehension in me. Every time, even if I was just a visitor. I guess that more than the structure itself I dreaded most the images it held within, the things a hospital stood for in my eyes, pain and suffering, the sorrow of broken hearts and broken bodies. That last sentinel for so many, separating life and death. In reality it is so much more. I see that now in my longing for a salvation, a cure that only a hospital can give to me. I am lucky this time—lucky even to have this hospital hope for the future. The accident could have been worse—I could be partially paralyzed by a shattered back, in a deep coma with blood oozing from my battered brain. Much worse. I imagine that someday in the future I will look back upon all this like some long-forgotten childhood nightmare and laugh at it. Together we'll laugh, Harley and I, for our foolishness, for what fools we have been.

Four-thirty-eight. Night has fallen already in the jungle valleys below. Darkness quickly creeps up the mountainside upon me. I gaze out through the blackness, down over humped moraines, searching, listening for a sign of the rescue party, the flicker of their blazing lamps far below or the faint metallic rattling of their gear sifting up to me on the gentle breeze. But there is nothing, no sign. My reaction to their absence is total acceptance. Surely I am buoyed still by confidence of impending rescue, but I am surprised. From within there wells up none of the normal feelings I might have expected: disappointment, wariness, disheartenment. I can muster not a tinge of concern. Sitting in the blackness, I wonder why I am so at ease now, so at peace. It is as if the subconscious protective instinct, ever on guard, has somehow lost its signal of communication with mind and body, a mind and body now flaccid, uncaring, incapable of emotion. I sink into a marshmallowy apathy. I am so tired now. Perhaps it is this exhaustion from the past days catching up with me, that creates these feelings. Yes, I must sleep. I switch on my headlamp to organize for another night, then cast the light in the direction of my companion watcher to see if he is still there. In random search for him, the golden beam cuts the cover of darkness. Behind the veil of falling flakes I see him caught in the sphere of illumination. Still he sits hunched upon his boulder, gaze fixed on me. Even in this spotlight I can't discern his features any more distinctly, only the drab gray outline of a man. "Hello again," I say to him good-naturedly. "Want some water?" I am compelled to try to draw him out. Perhaps he may tip his hand; I may resolve this mystery surrounding him. He does not respond. Settled in for the night, I switch out my headlamp. Across the darkness I say to him, "Don't catch your death o' cold now. We'll talk tomorrow—perhaps you'll feel more like it then." I have long since given up guessing the likes of this creature. Whatever he is, I suspect he is of little threat to me. In fact, I am beginning to like him, although I can't say he would be the life of the party. Well, I'll let him do the rest of the watching tonight. Serenely I sink into sleep. Enough, enough of this place. Away I must be.

Detached from self I soar upward over the continent of Africa. The wall of the Breach dissolves beneath me into insignificance, disappearing into the horizon, behind me, forgotten. Canyons, grassy plains, deserts, valleys, rain forests, blur beneath me on my journey. Past the rocky escarpment of the Gkarpo Mountains, the undulating ripples of the Namib Desert, the searing white salt plains of Etasha, the thunderous falls of Victoria, northward I stream, faster than any jet, over ten thousand square miles of lush green vegetation. Far below in a small clearing a figure signals me with a waving of arms. I descend. It is an old woman standing in the doorway of her small jungle hut. Silently she beckons me to enter. Slight, stooped over, this woman is ancient, with hair as white as snow and skin so weathered and bleached I cannot tell if she is white or black. Inside I settle into a small cane rocker. She hands me a cup of sweet tea and a great rectangular picture book. It is about East Africa. I scan the pages: the bubbling caldron of Lake Natron, lions, zebras, giraffes, roaming upon the shimmering plains of Serengeti, the black, symmetrical cinder cone of Lengai volcano brooding beneath blue heavens. Such beauty! Each photograph is more stunning than the last. Hippos bobbing about in Lake Naivasha. The precipitous somber walls of Hellsgate gorge. Fantastic! Now I turn the page to see a photo, out of place, vaguely familiar. Two feet stand upon a sandy Mombasa beach. Behind, the rolling azure surf of the Indian Ocean crashes in thunderous waves of white foam. Toes upon toes upon toes overlap and run diagonally across the page. My eyes search the multi-image in puzzlement. What can this mean? On the bottom of the page I discover the caption: "Rob Taylor's Toes." A moment's blur and suddenly I am in Mombasa. I walk along that beach in the brilliant sunshine. The air is warm and heavy. A sultry, idle breeze blows on shore, dancing in the palm fronds overhead. With each step my feet sink deep into the fine white sand, glimmering hot, yet wonderful to feel. I wiggle my toes amidst the particles, digging them deep into the moist cooler sand below. Ahhh! It feels so good. There's no pain, no pain anymore.

From the murky depth an alarm is sounded. A message sent. Slowly it trickles to my sleeping mind, trying to arouse it from its slumber. Drowsily I wiggle my toes. Yes, the pain, it's gone at last. More minutes of sleepy, relaxed contentment pass. I am suspended in that dreamy state somewhere between deep sleep and awake, drifting along. Again I wiggle my toes. No pain. At last the alarm registers: Nothing! I bolt upright in the blackness, wide awake. "I can't feel them," I say softly to the indifferent night. My skin prickles with the rushed release of adrenalin. My pulse and breathing quicken in fear. I can't feel anything! Groveling in the darkness for my headlamp, I find it and switch it on. Furiously I tear at the bivouac sack to get at my foot. Unzipping my sleeping bag, I am overwhelmed by a stench. The smell of death. It is bad. So bad, I suck in quick shallow gasps through my mouth to escape the odor, gagging incessantly. What could have brought about such a change in only hours? I fear the worst, frantically stripping off the splint, pushing aside the bloodstained padding and strapping, unlacing the boot, gently as possible trying to ease it from my foot, fingertips pushing against the leather collar of the boot top. This meager pressure releases renewed stabs of pain in the leg, but toes and foot remain insensible.

I panic, bearing down hard upon the boot, oblivious to the pain. Then harder still with all my might. It will not budge. The past heavy bleeding has dried firmly now, bonding the boot to my foot. Grasping my ice ax in hand, I hack at the boot, sinking the serrated pick deep into the counters. I use its shaft as a lever, grunting against the hardened creaking leather. Bit by bit I pry it open. After much struggling it releases its grip at last. The boot comes off. Still I have no answer. My foot remains entombed in three blood-saturated socks now hardened to a brittle red cement casing. With determined desperation, one by one I shred them against the spike of my ice ax and peel them off. The heavy outer sock goes quickly; the second more slowly. Like discarded shells of some deep-sea crustacean they lie on the snow beside me, each a form, a reproduction of my foot in every detail, yet without life, empty, hollow, cold. Was this my foot's fate, now hidden beneath that final sock? Gingerly I set about perforating it, taking care not to stab the spike into insensible flesh below. My arms ache with the effort, soon trembling uncontrollably. It is a tedious process requiring a steadiness of hand almost beyond me now. At last the sock is fully split top to toe. I begin peeling it away. The last point of adherence is directly over the wound. Try as I may, the sock will not be coaxed off lightly. After minutes of useless fidgeting, I sense there is but one way to remove it. Tattered sock in hand, I close my eyes, hold back a breath and rip it away. Lungs heave out, ears ring with a throaty scream. It is a God-blessed channel to pour out and release pain. I open my eyes to jets of steaming yellow pus exiting from the wound. Pressurized, it pulses forth in bursts down my foot onto the snow beside me, as if this vile substance has replaced life's blood in my veins. And the odor is as foul as it is inescapable.

Hunched over in the darkness, I grasp my left leg and hoist it toward my face. My eyes follow the shifting beam of the headlamp from lower calf to toes. I sigh in relief. It is better than I had hoped for, especially with the wound so severely infected. Ankle, foot, toes, though swollen and gray, are still very much alive. They show no signs of decay. Even as I hold my leg and examine it, the prickling needles of sensation return. Pallid skin flushes pink with renewed blood flow. I am elated. My foot had swelled within the confines of its boot until the tightness cut off all circulation and deadened all feeling. I envision the grim scene that would have greeted me by morning had I not awakened. Surely it would have been too late for my foot's survival. But what woke me? Was it my companion watcher? Was he sent to me as a messenger? This is the second good omen from his presence. Momentarily I search the darkness for him. I cannot find him. Whatever the reason, I am lucky. It is more than luck, though. I know it. I am not an aimless castaway idly adrift in destiny's backwaters, drawn by chance tides. Someone, some being, guides me on my journey. To a destination I know not yet. But never have I felt His hand so strongly. It gives me strength.

I set about to clean the ankle wound, groping on the dark ground around me for material I can use as makeshift dressing. Finding nothing, I resort to the left sleeve of my pile jacket. I slice it off at the shoulder junction, quite proficient now with my ice-ax cutter. I rip open the fabric tube along the seam, end to end, then fashion a dozen or so three-by-three-inch gauzelike pads out of it. I dab at the wound, amazed at its insensitivity. There's only a trace of feeling but a profusion of pus. Pad after pad I thrust into the wound, soaking them to saturation with the viscous yellow discharge, then casting them aside. Eventually I get down to glimpses of pink flesh. More time, continued daubing, and even small trickles of fresh red blood appear. A welcome sight: a wound at last looking as it should look, red, raw, bloody. As I rub away, the irony hits me: I am actually happy to see blood. How many other times would a person rejoice at such a sight?

Soon satisfied with my efforts, I place the few remaining pile patches over the wound, then pad and resplint the ankle. I mound the pumice beneath the foot of the bivy sack to a rounded hump. The elevation will keep the swelling in my injured foot to a minimum and hinder infection's spread. I settle once more into the warmth of my sleeping bag, realizing as I snuggle in that the one thing that my body craves most just now is the worst thing for my leg. The warm moist air trapped within the sleeping bag is an excellent breeding ground for bacteria, the perfect climate for infection to flourish. I reach down and zip open a small slit in the foot section of the bag, pushing my splinted ankle out to cooler air, yet leaving it still protected by the outer skin of the bivy sack. It is a matter of temperature regulation now to maximize the chances of saving the leg. By pushing the leg out more, the temperature near the foot further drops, inhibiting germs' growth. But it must not get too cold lest the cells, the foot itself, freeze and the tissue die. Nor can the foot be drawn too close to the warmth of the sleeping bag, for this would incite infection's rapid growth once more, which in only a matter of hours could devour the life of my leg, perhaps my life. A compromise must be sought. But what is it? What is the right position for the foot? The right temperature? Success now is but a whim that blows upon the wind, rustling the falling snow. An inch or two shifts all of the weight on the scales of health. I move my leg outward. Too far. Pull it in. Too near. Place it between the two, then push it out again. After frustrating minutes of adjusting, assured of no perfect placement, I settle my foot in a spot where the toes are chilly but not numb, and hope for the best.

Before lying back I cast the beam of my headlamp across the void to the usual place of my companion watcher. I will ask him. Perhaps this once he will answer me, tell me what is right to do. I search the night. Has he abandoned me? After so many hours of his staying by me so steadfastly, I've grown fond of this fellow, maybe even need him. Now he is gone and I am saddened. I've

2

3

7

8

relied on this being, whoever he is, more than I've cared to admit. Confidence shaken, I stare out into the darkness for some minutes as mind tries to reason with emotion. Then I see something, to the left, just at the perimeter of the field of light. It's he! "Hello! Where did you go? Where have you been?" As usual he does not answer. Surely he has moved. He seems much closer now. Yet when I focus in on him with the light, I see him no more clearly. I blink several times to clear away a gauzy film that obscures my sight. It remains. Perhaps he hasn't moved at all; it's only the darkness that distorts my perspective of him. In the boulder-strewn slope before me, every rock looks similar to every other, and I cannot begin to guess where he may have been before or where he has moved to now. What does it matter, anyway? He's here. I still have my foot. It is just before 3 A.M. I sink back heavily to the ground, exhausted, drained from the past hours. Soon I sleep again.

An ice peak looms on the horizon, an immense uncut diamond glittering brilliantly in the winter sunshine. Something draws me toward it. I cannot resist. I am compelled to go to it. The years of aimless wandering, roaming the breadth of the Scottish High-lands like some lost soul, are at an end. I have a goal: this peak. It strikes up high from the surroundings, like the fluted head of an arrow, the razor-honed tip of a spear. Upon the lower mountain flanks I dismount. I abandon my steed. Upward I clamber, tossing dirk and claymore to the ground behind me. I am a man driven on by some relentless call, a summons. Who could it be? What could they want? Ever higher I climb, and ever more treacherous becomes the terrain. The mountain is now but a windswept wasteland, tilted to the vertical. All things are veiled beneath the smothering shrouds of ice. With every additional step I fear more for my life. Repeatedly I falter, slipping from my holds, almost falling to my death. Still I continue my desperate upward struggle. Some magnetic allure from the summit pulls ever more strongly upon me. I must go on.

The slope eases. At last I pull up on the final ridge beneath the summit tower and into the full force of a raging gale. It tears at my frosted beard, ripping the tam from my head. I can barely stand against its buffeting. I gather the pleats of my woolen kilt close around me, but the wind drives the cold and the snow through the creases like knives. Crouched upon the ridge without shelter, I shiver uncontrollably, trying to rewarm my deadened senses. Then I hear it. "Rob!" It is only a whisper, yet carried by this wind it roars in the ears like the call of a thousand uplifted voices. Again. "Rob." I spin around into the wind. There upon the slender curving ridge of the summit a figure stands, not fifty feet away. It is a man in the black-and-blue kilt of the Stewarts, tartan of our murdered Queen Mary, God rest her soul. The wind-driven pellets of ice raise stinging welts upon my face, but I hardly attend to them. I recognize the figure. "Davey!" I shout. "You're alive! You're not dead!" In this roaring wind I hear no response from him, yet he motions me with the wave of his arm to follow. He turns and moves toward the summit. Madly I rush upon the ridge to pursue him. I climb as fast as I can. In the maze of ice-glazed steps and blocks, somehow I lose sight of him. When finally I break out on the small flat rectangular summit, no larger than a tabletop, he is not there. Nothing is. Sheer walls fall away on all sides, all except for the one ridge whence I have just come. It's impossible. Where could he have gone? Deceived, desperate now, I scream to the howling heavens, "David! Where are you? Come back!" There is nothing. Tired, exhausted, I slump to the ground. I can go on no longer now. I have not the strength to retreat back down this mountain. I shall die here, alone, on this peak. I gaze out through rime-encrusted eyes into space, awaiting my end. Then I see him again—Dave. Beyond the summit he stands suspended in the sky, a glory in the air, beckoning to me again with the wave of his arm to follow after him. I shiver. I'm so cold I cannot move, but my body quivers with wave after wave of shivering.

Shivering, I awaken, cold, drenched with perspiration, even my sleeping bag soaked. Its wet, clammy nylon sticks against my skin as I try to shake the sleep from my mind. I raise a hand to my forehead. It burns hot with fever. So drained am I of energy that it is a task to lift my head and check the time: 6:17. But is that A.M. or P.M? It's still dark out, but is it the blackness of night or the fast-fading darkness of approaching first light? I search my memory for some clue. Three A.M. was the time at last check. I've been dreaming. David! In the past four years I have thought of him often, yet never had he figured in a single dream. Why does he haunt me now? I wonder. His friendship is a comfort even across the boundary of death. Why was he signaling me to follow, and there, far beyond the summit? Is it that our friendship is death's passageway and Dave my guide? Perhaps death was not the grisly hyena of the first part of Hemingway's story, but rather the airplane journey of the ending, a ride with a friend to greater heights.

Within the hour the snow-filled dawn of January 18 arises, pale, gray, lackluster. It brings no respite, no joy. Down over the moraines, now blanketed white, I see nothing. Each day since Harley's departure, I have kept this vigil. I awaited the arrival of a rescue party with continued confidence and hope. I convinced myself that any second now they would appear below, just a few more minutes, I would see them. Ever did I fill my idle time devising reasons for the delays, Harley's in reaching them and theirs in returning. Now the minutes have turned to hours and the hours to days. With the gray light of this morning comes also the grim realization: help is not coming. Period. There is no question in my mind now that some catastrophe has befallen Harley. It is simply a matter of by what means he met his end—devoured by a leopard, fallen off a cliff, hopelessly lost in the maze of rain forest, felled by hypothermia. Any of them, all of them, are too plausible. Harley is gone. Dead, I am certain of it. Was it I who sent him to his death? I realize now that in only hours I will join him, perishing in this spot.

I lie in the gently falling snow, acceptance of my fate coming slowly. I wonder how many untold numbers of men have felt the mountain's lure and succumbed to it, only to meet their end upon its lofty flanks. Many I know. But why? What elusive prize did we seek? What reward of spirit surpassing life itself? Perhaps now in death I would have the answer. Death. Harley and I never shared a word about it. I had seen so much of it in mountain rescue. Broken battered bodies. It used to make me sick at first. Then I just got used to it. I tried never to learn their names or recognize their faces. It was too painful. They were just other lads who got the chop. Now Harley and I join this corps of climbers, just so much rotting compost on the hillside. Separated, alone; not a being in the world marks our passing. No tears of grief shall be shed for us. No prayers murmured. There is only the companion watcher. I look over to him. There he sits, ever aloof, chin in hand, elbow on knee. He is closer now, yet the snow around him remains untracked. Will he wait till the end?

After so many days of fighting, struggling to survive, enduring the pain, with success almost at hand, suddenly it is over. Avalanches, storms, rockfall, the mountain did not defeat us, Harley and me. We had defeated ourselves. First in spirit up on the Wall. Now in body. We failed. One might say that time, good fortune, luck just ran out on us. But perhaps this is the way it was always meant to end. I am not bitter. The stolid presence of my companion watcher impresses upon me the fact that no one ever promised me that life and death would be an equitable proposition. I lived my entire life as if it were a game of chance, continually balancing on that thin thread between life and death. Now, as it draws to a close, I may desire to quit the game, to change the rules. I cannot. Before my eyes life slips from my grasp. Life, I see now, was never mine to keep, only to hold for a time. I feel no anger or indignation. They are futile. It is only a matter of time . . . awaiting the end.

In silent contemplation my mind strikes out and wanders at will through a memory of twenty-three years. There is no wild grief for want of a twenty-fourth, just muted sadness. It is not so bad an end. I die in the place, doing the thing, I cherish most. Mountains and climbing. I will remain with them eternally now. Other images of the past, fleeting random images, click by my mind's eye.

Liberty Ledge, the old farm. A mass of open rolling emerald hills bordered by deep, dark forests. Forests of white pine that soared straight as an arrow high overhead. At one time, they said, wolves and bears lived in the woods. They said that Old Lou had even killed one when he was a young man, but that was long before I was born. Still I always envisioned running into one of them as I wandered the dim canyon beneath the canopy of the treetops. It was exciting, frightening, to imagine it might be true. In the small house of knotty pine devised by my grandfather, Papa, life had begun for me. What a place! More cabin than house, it was a structure he had built years earlier without plans or measurements, just one board nailed to another till it all came together. It creaked and groaned with each shift of the wind; drafts of cold air whistled through every nook and cranny those early years. It was all we had, it and the land. We loved it—so much so, it was all the house my family would ever want, even later when there was more money. As a child I spent literally years looking at the walls and the ceiling, searching out knots. There were thousands of them. Paired together they became sets of coal-black eyes staring out at me, of every type imaginable. There were Japanese eyes, pirate eyes, angry eyes, happy eyes, Indian eyes, and crying eyes. Night's darkness brought more than its share of nightmares those years as a multitude of eyes, good and evil, stared down at me. They watched me through the blackness even when I couldn't see them.

Home. The name itself holds so much feeling, so many

memories. It is hard to believe I will never return, not glimpse its beauty or draw a single breath of its wondrous smells. Not even embrace my family one last time, if only for assurance. I regret this most. The weeks ahead will be filled with sorrow and pain for them when they hear the news, learn of my fate. Was it fair to make them suffer so? Have I been selfish? If only I could ease their acceptance, make them understand. Tell them everything is fine. I wonder how Dave and Johnny felt about leaving their loved ones behind. That August day, Dave's little girl was but six months old. And Johnny. He'd gone leaving his wife, Ali, two small mouths to feed and an infant who would never know his father. Did they carry a sense of remorse beyond with them?

My family. They are strong. When confronted by such a trial, they will bond together and be stronger still. In the end I am certain they will come to accept my death just as they came to accept my life, my mountains, my climbing, the things that besides them I loved most. Always they supported me, stood behind me one hundred percent, even if they did not fully fathom the passion that drew me to the heights.

Now I hope, no, expect, that someday they will realize a deeper understanding of my life, of my death; for it was through them that the seeds of my love of mountains were sown and subsequently flourished. They instilled in me a deep appreciation for living—that essence of life. Those dewy spring morns all bright and sunwashed. By eight, my grandmother is already hard at work, on hands and knees, amidst her flowers. All colors of the garden swell around her, a bounty of scents perfuming the morning air. She gives each blossom, every plant its due care as if she knows exactly what they desire, where they wish to reside in the flower bed. Most of all, though, her attentions go to the heathers—two immense sprawling mounds, one on either front side of her cottage. I could not understand her in those early days. To me heather was ugly, straggly woody tufts of weeds devoid of any beauty. Over the years I saw I was wrong. Nana in her usual unspoken way opened my eyes to the subtle intricate beauties of the heather, its minute fragile blossoms. With time I grew to realize that for Nana this heather was more than a plant. It was a tie to another time, to another place, a bond that she would never allow to be broken.

The hazy days of summer. We arise with the dawn at five or earlier. Even in the early-morning hours the air hangs heavy with the sweet smell of the hayfield's first cutting. This is the season of life, and Papa my guide to its wonders. In the garden the seeds he plants will yield a hundredfold of squash, over two hundred bushels of tomatoes. But there is so much more he shows me. At the barn we collect eggs from the henhouse. Under his watchful eye we candle them before a light. Into two piles we separate them. Some will be eaten, the remainder go into the small round incubator. In only days egg becomes chick. The miracle of life.

Autumn, and the days grow shorter. They are highlighted by a sprinkling of crimson maples in a sea of green pines. On the farm it is never falling leaves, a cascade of colors, but falling pine needles. Like brown sleet they sweep down from the treetops. In only days they mound up thick upon the ground. Pine beds set down like quilts for winter's warmth. As a child I often sprang along their cushioning mat, breathing deeply their rich earthy aroma. Fall, as much as I loved it, always brought a certain sadness. Nature's season of dying. Not only for flowers, plants, crickets, and butterflies, but as well for sheep, cattle, chickens. Animals so lovingly cared for over the months. The morning they took the three Highland blackface I could scarcely believe they would never return. Only months old. Chris cried. That afternoon men loaded plastic bags of meat into our truck. Alba, my mother, whom we call Al, tried to explain. It was a difficult task. She said these animals had given their lives for us so that we might continue to live through the winter. It seemed a cruel reality, to eat one's pets, but somehow she had made us understand. Understanding—this is certainly Al's greatest resource. It runs as deep as the ocean and is just as vast. For all my days she nurtured and instilled in me a deep respect for life . . .

and death. She will take my death the hardest, yet pull the strongest to get the family over it.

Winter brings its pristine blanket of white, smothering autumn's bleakness for a time. Snow. To my mind nothing matches its beauty and purity. After a heavy fall, it lies deep in the woods, nestled around every tree, smooth, untracked. But especially for my family, winter meant skiing. I was only four on my first ski trip. I tottered along on my skis through the dense snow-mantled conifers. Desperately I struggled, floundering in the deep powder to keep up with my brother and sister. It would be a few years yet before I would challenge them. Yes, Mark and Chris, what times we had as children! Years of discovery, tree forts, explorations, horseback riding, roaming fields and woods. Now never to return. Will the same be true of my spirit? Is it doomed to one place, here, for eternity? I implore God to let my spirit go. Allow it to roam free.

In the light of morning a darkness pours over me. A heavy black mist that at times obscures my vision. I am feverish. Am I hallucinating? Am I awake or dreaming? Thought, reality, apparition merge into one. No longer can I differentiate among them. Through the haze I look to my companion watcher for solace. He is gone. I scan the broken ground for his now so familiar silhouette. He stands now at the foot of my bivouac sack, gray, somber, motionless. Is he truly there? I am confused. Behind him, over his shoulder, I see David, and beyond, others—Ian, Dougal, Johnny. They are whole. They live once more. Silently they gesture to me: Come! "But where?" I whisper. Again, they only gesture: Come! "I can't. I can't move. I must wait here." They turn to move away. "Hey, wait! Don't go!" I call to them, but the rift between us widens. At last I jump up to follow after them, then suddenly remember my gear. "Hold on just a second!" I turn to grab it. I am frozen midmotion, mouth agape. A body lies there—there in my yellow bivouac sack, where I have just been. Vacant eyes stare outward from an ashen face, gaunt and stiff. I lean over to touch the skin.

It is icy cold. There is no warmth left in this spent vessel. Staring closely at this shattered shell of a man, I recognize him. "It's me!" I turn and run after my comrades lest I lose them. The companion watcher leads the way. Rapidly we bound up the slopes toward the crest of the Window Buttress. Suddenly I realize—my leg! Looking down, I see two legs, normal, vibrant, healthy. What was it, now, about my leg? I can't seem to remember.

Upon the rock prow of the Window Buttress I turn and look back upon the infinite white slopes, back at the small golden blotch upon the snow far below. It is farewell.

X

Please!
Come take my hand
Carry me home
Across this land

The faintest of sounds wafts stealthily into this unworldly province I now inhabit. Again I hear it, an unwanted meddler intruding into my consciousness. It pulls me back. Back down the passage through which I have just come. I resist. But it compels me to return. Now the crystalline sphere of my vision seams with a multitude of hairline fractures like the veined surface of some porcelain vessel. Quickly the minute cracks separate, expanding into disjointed fissures, growing ever wider, until resolved into empty blackness. Try as I may I lose sight of the companion watcher, of Dave, of all my friends. Once more I am blind to that "other" ethereal realm. I open my eyes and the vision is earthly: the cold white of eternal snow. My mind returns to a reality of hope, of wanting to survive, to live.

My ears prick. I listen for more sound. So many times in the past days I've seen and heard things—or have wished them—only to be disappointed later. Now I strain to listen over the light wailing wind. It sounds again! I swear I hear my name being called. Glancing across the scree, I look to my companion watcher. He is vanished. Yet the sound continues to grow in volume and intensity. Soon I can make out a distinct "Rob, Rob, Rob, Rob." The word has never sounded so sweet. My own return shouts of "HELLOOOOO" are quickly answered. My heart pounds with anticipation. Back and forth this exchange continues for a half an hour, yet I can see no one through the fluttering curtain of white. Finally from below there appears on top of a sloping whale-backed ridge a tall silhouette, black against the snow-covered terrain. It stands motionless, statuesque, for several minutes. Its complete lack of movement is unsettling, convincing me it is but another mirage. Yet just as my hope slackens, the figure breaks into a stride, quickly moving in my direction. Some distance behind, another dark silhouette comes into view, and another, then another. A rescue party has truly come. The minutes between sighting and arrival stretch to eternity. My eyes strain to keep the slowly upward-moving figures constantly in view, as I lean forward on my elbows, convinced that I control and will their destiny and that to lose sight of them, for just one instant, will cause them to disappear, cease to exist. But I keep watch and they do not fade.

Up out of the heavily falling snow staggers a tall gaunt figure, clad in red, with deep piercing blue eyes and hair the color of bleached straw. From the altitude and the long hours of exertion he is breathless, tired. As he wipes the streams of sweat from his face with his sleeve he forces his questions in between gasps for air. "Rob," he stammers forcibly in uneven, heavily accented English, "I am Odd Eliassen. We were so worried we will find you dead. How are you? How is your leg?"

Staring up at his haggard, lined, and sunburned face, I see the countenance of a man overwrought by concern—with indescribable intensity. I find it difficult to believe that my ordeal is over. Odd tells me that at the outset of this rescue mission he doubted it was to be anything but a body recovery; yet always he kept a small pocket of hope, knowing from his own mountain experiences on Everest, in Russia, and in Norway how strong and resilient the human spirit could be. Now his brow unfurrows and his wrinkles run into a wide smile as he sees I am still alive. Yet the gravity of the situation is all too apparent to both of us. I shiver and burn with fever. The wound's infection has spread and is now entrenched in my system. I am severely dehydrated and weak. And on top of this, there still lies before us more than seventy-five miles of travel before the nearest hospital can be reached, much of it overland by foot and through jungle. We realize it will take both speed and luck if we are to save this leg of mine. Odd radios park headquarters, saying he has found me alive. He relates to them his intent to begin evacuation within the half hour.

The remainder of the rescue party, five native rangers from Mount Kilimanjaro National Park, arrive stragglingly with the medical supplies. Silently they gather round Odd, watchful. The contrast between them and him is striking. In the radiant, reflected light I can distinguish no trace of features upon any of the rangers' dark faces. There are simply oval black holes staring out at me where their visages should be. I am not able to garner the slightest hint of their emotions, or their feelings toward me, positive or negative. They remain distant, unknown, alien. It is unsettling.

Odd urgently removes the old dressing, casting it aside, and sets about cleaning the wound. The stench of the purulent drainage from the open weeping ankle makes him cringe to fight off the urge to vomit. But on he works steadfastly, determined. With every daub of the antiseptic cloth into the wound, he winces, finding it incredible that I feel nothing of his scrubbing. When Odd explains he has brought no antibiotics, the one major item I stressed to Harley I needed most, I blanch in desperation. "How can this be ?" The doctor from whom Odd received the medical supplies would not issue any; he said, "Antibiotics given now could be lethal!" He assured Odd, "As long as the wound is kept open and draining, everything will be fine." Torn between explosive anger and overwhelming disappointment, I brood silently for a few minutes. No, I have passed up the consolation of despair too many times to give in now. I will not forsake hope. I force myself to believe I will make it.

Odd rolls on the final bandages, explaining to me as best he can the reason for the delay. Harley decided against going to the Horombo Hut as he and I had agreed; instead he trekked down into the rain forest, got lost, and arrived at the very base of the mountain thirty-six hours after he set out. Odd received word of the accident only the previous evening at 7 P.M. We cannot understand Harley's decision to take the longer route, and Odd reiterates how sorry he is I have been left so long. Considering the output required for Odd and the rescue team to reach me in only fourteen hours, I realize that apologies are unnecessary. Only thanks and gratitude on my part are called for.

I sit in the snow drinking hot tea, the warmth fast returning to my body, happy to be alive. I say to myself, "What does it matter now, I have rescuers. Finally my private ordeal is over." Once again I had mistaken the close of a chapter for the end of a book. As two of the rangers, using a small gas stove, heat and cure my newly fitted splint, which Odd has fashioned out of numerous plaster roller-bandages, the remainder gather up and repack the gear for our departure.

Over the past half hour or so, I sensed that something here was unusual . . . amiss. Yet I am not able to put my finger on it. Odd kneels beside me and produces from his pocket several glass amber-filled ampules and a metallic cylinder, much like the tubes cigars come in.

"Rob, you must take some morphine," he states questioningly.

"What? Now?" I counter defensively. "After so many days so far without it?" I assure him that I don't want any, nor will I need any for the stretcher ride that remains.

His response comes softly, calmly, but carries with it the force of a right hook. "Rob, there is no stretcher. We will carry you on our backs."

Dazed by this response, I turn over his words in my mind in disbelief. "No stretcher?" The stretcher is the element that is missing here! No one said there was one; I just assumed it. Everywhere I have helped in carrying the injured down out of the mountains, the stretcher was an essential piece of equipment. In fact, the words "rescue" and "stretcher" were almost synonymous to me. Here this was a foolish assumption. On this side of Kilimanjaro they simply do not have one.

Realizing the jolting and jarring that my leg would soon be subjected to, I submit feebly to Odd's directive. He snaps the glass neck off the ampule, loads the syringe, and hesitantly eases the needle into my right arm. As he squeezes out the morphine, his eyes nervously dart back and forth between mine and the syringe. When it is emptied and withdrawn, Odd lets out a long sigh of relief, repacking the syringe into its tube. He adds, "Rob, I hope it didn't hurt too much. This is the first I've ever given."

"I'd never have known. You did it just like a pro."

Odd relishes the compliment, a smile sparkling on his face. Amazing. Here is a man who has just brought a rescue team to over sixteen-thousand feet in only fourteen hours, and he is more pleased by his nursing success than by this feat of endurance.

Within minutes I feel the results. With the deadening of the pain in my leg comes a bone-tingling chill. Quickly it spreads from fingertips to toes throughout my body. As the narcotic surges, I have the sensation of being plucked up and swept away into the swirling mainstream of a vast river. I can only imagine to what thundering abyss this current will carry me. Perception dulled and blurred, my eyes view my surroundings as if through a fog or from beneath the surface of a placid pool. Images and light bend and refract at odd angles, fuzzy and soft around the edges. I sit perfectly still upon the ground, yet it shifts and rolls about me like a wave. My power of concentration, my ability to focus on a simple thought for more than a few seconds, deserts me. In this realm, space and time are warped by another dimension. I shiver from the biting cold now pulsing through my veins.

Duly considering a number of different rescue methods, Odd decides upon the rope-coil shoulder carry as the quickest and most efficient. Yet as soon as I am loaded onto one of the ranger's backs, the impracticality of the method is obvious. The rangers are the better part of a foot shorter than myself. They find it impossible to keep their balance in the shifting snow while simultaneously trying to control the topheavy, tilting load I present on their shoulders. Alternately they trade places to give it a try. None save Odd and one other, Hubert, manages to stagger more than a few paces before collapsing. Unfortunately, Hubert is by far the shortest of the lot. So short that when I am upon his back my splinted leg, even when pulled up under tension, continually bumps and drags upon the ground. With each step I moan in pain despite the morphine.

Immediately Odd realizes this will not work. He scraps this technique as a possibility for the rangers, leaving the unenviable task only to himself. Carry after carry, he trudges downward several hundred yards at a stretch, driving himself to the limit. When nearly exhausted he surrenders me over to the rangers, whom he has divided into groups of two, allowing these teams to take up the burden while he rests. Working in pairs, the rangers manage me sufficiently, soon settling upon a feasible method of carry: the arm-support-hopping technique, in which I hang from the shoulders of two rescuers, hopping all the while on my right foot. In this way, step by step, we descend, each team carrying for ten minutes at a stretch before changing positions. Interspersed with Odd's speedy solitary carries, this maneuver is tediously slow on the shifting, uneven ground. It is also fatiguing, for although each of the pairs has a short respite, this procedure necessitates continual exertion on my part. The scene is surreal: a weary one-legged man races the fastest opponent of all, time!

Still, it is progress. Alternating among the three pairs and Odd's carries, we get into a regular, relatively efficient pattern, slowly descending hour upon hour throughout the afternoon. Steadily my strength and spirit weaken. With each renewed bout, I find my arms sooner and sooner in the course of a carry turning to rubber. Against my will, clasped fingers unbend, releasing their grip no matter how hard I wish them closed. Soon I won't be able to hold on.

Odd, sensing my pain, begins a barrage of small talk, continually drawing me into conversation, dropping in words of encouragement. This newfound friend's incessant banter about the mountains, interests we share, or the plotting of future exploits we will undertake together, all strive to take my mind off the present nightmare and quell within me the growing pangs of desperation. At length he speaks of his climbing trips to Mount Everest in Nepal, the Hindu Kush, and Russia; and of his experiences ski touring in Iran and Turkey. Then we compare notes as to our favorite locations in Norway. Odd's are the isles of Lofoten, mine the mountains of Jotunheimen. Places we yet long to visit: he, Kashmir; I, Antarctica. He assures me, regardless of how serious the situation may be now, we will yet have many good times together in the mountains. His infectious optimism rekindles in me the fire of life. I believe him!

Upon the final slopes of the Heim Moraine, which swoop down severely below us to disappear into the headwall of the Window Buttress, the going bogs down. So steep and unconsolidated are these mammoth wavelike dunes of pumice, it is difficult to descend them in a standing position alone without falling over backward. For a linked trio, it is nigh impossible. The ground shifts like quicksand under our feet. In our urgent efforts to make headway, we look like driving pistons, unevenly sinking down, rising up, sinking down. We get nowhere. I recall a similar experience years before on a rescue in Glencoe, when Hamish used a sleeping bag as a sled to lower a casualty over a slope of steep, soft, bottomless snow. It worked so well then that I now suggest using my large yellow bivouac sack as the makeshift sled. I lie squarely in the center of the sheet, on my back, head downhill to keep the injured leg elevated and protected, while Odd strategically places rangers round the perimeter. The front men are to be the accelerators; the rear, the brakemen. Off we set, sluggish at first, but then quickly gathering speed as the nylon swishes over the smooth surface, barely on the verge of control. The rangers leap wildly downhill in pursuit, struggling to keep up. In only a matter of minutes we are at the top of the buttress, gazing back up at a slope that would have otherwise taken hours to descend.

On the Window Buttress we retrace the route Harley and I took earlier. In my present state, however, negotiating the same steep ground we passed over so quickly, so easily, on our ascent requires the utmost effort and attention now. The route lies down a number of interconnected down-sloping ledges, some no greater than a foot wide, which seam the Window Buttress into tier upon tier of cliff bands up to a total height of a thousand feet.

Like mice trying to negotiate an immense vertical maze, we feel our way along, seeking a booty more valuable than some bit of cheese. For a well-bodied mobile individual, this route if taken slowly with a little care presents no problem or danger, except for a bit of apprehension from the yawning exposure at one's feet. To us, however, it is a major impediment, gradually squeezing off our progress to a crawl. With each additional step the danger of a fall becomes greater. Yet we have no alternative. Cautiously we edge downward, wondering how long we will be able to grope our way on this ever narrowing ledge, barely the width of one person but forced to accommodate me and two bearers.

In minutes we are brought to a full stop. Ahead the ledge peters out entirely into a smooth near-vertical precipice, broken only by two small rock holds several feet apart. It is impossible to cross this sheer expanse by our present method. There is only one choice. I must climb down the wall under my own power, just as I did from high on the Breach, utilizing my hands and my good foot on the holds. I am so weak I wonder if I still have the strength. As a safeguard, Odd secures me with a backup rope from above belayed by one of the rangers. Odd at my shoulder pointing out the way, I labor inch by inch across and downward, lunging from handhold to foothold. I am thankful for the rope this day. I hang from it exhausted every several meters, trying to regain some energy. More than once I slip, begin to fall, only to be pulled up taut by the rope and saved. Every slip, every incipient fall, brings flashbacks of another fall and another rope. The yank of this rope jars me back to reality.

When we are only several hundred feet from the bottom of the buttress, a large noisy band of German TV personnel in the area making a documentary on Kilimanjaro come up to meet us. I am at first puzzled, then utterly bewildered by this visitation of harlequins clad in the most fashionable of shiny new caps, jackets and trousers in every color of the rainbow, clambering across the barren rock-strewn barrancos. It is a chance meeting of two worlds, each totally alien to the other. One, inhabited by dirty, filthy, stinking creatures, fighting and struggling for life itself. The other, by individuals whose perfect, painted countenances reflect the light and whose bodies are pressed into sterile brightly colored plastic, radiating the most enticing of scents. Pure pleasure!

Cameras in hand, they jibber, jabber, and gesticulate at Odd like animated wind-up toys, firing a dozen interrogations and declarations at him simultaneously. My quizzical glance at Odd to find out "What the hell is going on?" is met with only the most pathetic of tired, forlorn faces.

"These Germans," he says, "insist on helping us carry, at least as far as the Barranco Boulder. It's impossible to talk to them. They won't listen." Considering how dog-tired every man of the rescue team is, Odd can do little but accept their offer. In fact, the Germans probably would carry out their "rescue" regardless of his wishes, one way or another. Better to accept.

Zealously the Germans sling me over their backs, carrying me a short distance, passing me like so many pounds of sacked potatoes from one to another. Odd looks on helplessly at their steady bickering and arguing among themselves. His entreaties of "Watch Out! Be careful!" go unheeded. They seem impervious to the fact that I am still alive, impervious to my groans of pain as time and again they hit, bump, knock, and step on my shattered leg. Several times I am dumped sprawling to the ground as my "rescuer" collapses on top of me. As with many erring people when confronted with a fellow human in suffering, the urge to help is mistaken for the ability to do so. Arrival at the Barranco Boulder leaves me appreciative of their good intentions but thankful this parody is finally ended.

Odd originally hoped that an air evacuation could be undertaken this day from here by government helicopter. But mist and heavy clouds have set in as the afternoon progressed, and now, just minutes after we are under shelter, the skies open, venting their wrath in angry torrents. There will be no helicopter today. The Germans scurry for the shelter of their round silver-metallic tents perched upon the desolate land like docked alien spaceships. We shall spend the night here beneath the Barranco Boulder. The underside of the boulder is a steeply arched concave roof rising up to over twenty feet at the lip of the entrance. From here the hollow sinks back into the very bowels of this immense solitary shard of rock for more than fifteen feet. It is here we find snug, dry refuge.

The dull, flat gray of afternoon dwindles languidly into night. Odd lights a fire with wood he and the rangers have carried up from the forest below, and several of the rangers begin cooking dinner. They roast small chickens skewered onto the picks of their ice axes over the fire, while the remainder tend pots of beans and maize set into the coals. The flames roar upward, bolts of yellow-green light fueled by the dripping chicken grease. The wafting charcoal scent of the singed meat draws every man to the fire in hungry anticipation. All save me. I am too fatigued to move closer. For me tiredness of body wins out over enthusiasm of mind and senses. I remain watching the rangers several yards off huddled round the pulsing blaze. Softly they whisper to one another in rhythmic staccato bursts of Swahili, occasionally breaking out into fits of loud giggling. The flickering flames light up their faces, and for the first time clearly I see individual features. This past day's long puzzlement—faceless names being called out, filling my ears time and again: Athanasi . . . Hubert . . . Karlo, names not of personalities but of visageless black holes—is finished. I see them. Athanasi, with his narrow oval face furrowed in seriousness. William-Francis, quiet, serene, the picture of cherubic innocence. Hubert, great round moon face grinning ear to ear, endlessly trying (without success) to subdue his giddiness. The rangers are people now.

When it comes time to eat, I have no desire for food. In fact, the mere thought of it repels me. Odd is insistent. "Rob, you must eat!" Eventually I do force down some warm bouillon and tea. Later, before he turns in, Odd strongly advises I take one last injection of morphine to help me get some much-needed rest and sleep. Neither of us knows what tomorrow may bring. Wholeheartedly I agree. Injection given, quickly the morphine takes effect. I pull up close to the deep-red glowing embers of the dying fire and melt into relaxed drowsiness. Pain and reality are once more shuttered away. As I am lulled into a deep sleep, golden gossamers entwine my body and spirit me away.

During the night, two more rangers arrive carrying an old army-surplus stretcher borrowed from the Moshi hospital. It seems relatively insignificant now that so much of the difficult terrain has already been covered. Still, whatever tomorrow brings, at least from here on I can be carried.

The sun is long risen through broken clouds before any of us awakens. The ranger Athanasi is first up, yet it is neither the sun nor the light that rouses him. It is the sound of a distant droning. He yells, "Listen! Mr. Eliassen . . . *Listen!*," startling us all awake. In seconds we are fully attentive. We lie in our sleeping bags holding our breath, ears straining. Then we all hear it, too, the droning! And it steadily grows louder.

Odd leaps from bed, swearing, "Oh my God—shit! The helicopter!" Shoving away all his gear, he barks frantic orders at the sleepy rangers, "Come on, wake up! The helicopter is coming. Get Rob ready. Hurry up!" He speaks and the rangers spring to readiness. Grabbing his pack and my broken ice ax, Odd quickly sprints away up a nearby hill out of sight while the rangers load me on the stretcher. They strap me in securely, lift me onto their shoulders, and proceed up the hill.

Midway up the rise the steep angle eases back to nearly level, forming one small forty-foot step in the larger slope. On this patch of horizontal ground Odd comes into view, a blur of frenetic motion. Madly he runs about, ice ax in hand slashing and swiping wildly at any object over six inches in height, leveling the area like a golf fairway for our makeshift heliport.

Through the swirling mist down in the Umbwe Valley we see the helicopter at last, revolving upward in small elliptic circles, corkscrew fashion, straining to gain altitude in the thin air. It darts in and out of the clouds. In only minutes it will arrive.

While Odd finishes grading the interior area of the landing site, he orders the rangers to remove a nearby fifteen-foot giant groundsel which borders on the pad and may interfere with the landing of the chopper. I watch the rangers struggle with all their might to topple the thick rubbery stock of the plant. I cannot help laughing hysterically. The scene is like some irreverent reversal of the proud Marine flag-raising at Iwo Jima. Time and time again they violently shove it down, only to have it snap back shudderingly upright when they release their grip. It is a comical but fruitless routine. It takes Odd only several ax blows at its base to send it tumbling down. All is ready.

"Where is the helicopter?" he shouts. Directly in front of us the small transparent bubble of the chopper has momentarily been swallowed by the mist. Yet the sound draws ever closer. "Everyone look out for it," says Odd. "Watch for it to appear!"

With all eyes straining skyward to catch some glimpse of it, once again Athanasi sees first. Then we all see it, coming in just above eye level, straight on. "It's too low!" worries Odd. Closer and closer through the scattered mist it comes.

Suddenly, for no apparent reason, the chopper slows, hesitates, veers away rightward. In seconds it is gone. The pilot must have been afraid to approach any closer. Afraid of the mist and the clouds that obscured his vision and at any time could have overwhelmed him, leaving him to fly such delicate maneuvers completely blind, at an altitude already beyond the ceiling allowance of his helicopter. After a couple of tries, he decides it is just too chancy. The possibility of an airlift rescue fades with the receding drone of the chopper. Odd feels we can afford to wait no longer, wasting time for something that may never materialize. The rescue team will finish the carry off the mountain.

Perhaps because I held no false expectations or maybe because I had no time to build up any for an air rescue, whatever the reason, I feel little disappointment. Odd is surprised by my lack of reaction, my easy acceptance. But I am confident. I illogically convince myself that the additional hours will make little difference to my leg after so many days. Perhaps this is necessary to go on.

From our present location at the Barranco Boulder in the Umbwe Valley we are separated from the rescue vehicles by the gray hulking mass of the Shira Plateau which rises above us. To continue our descent off the mountain we must first make a steep climb of several thousand feet up to the plateau. We will then traverse this high-altitude plateau for some kilometers and at long last drop down a short distance to waiting transport. Everyone is heartened. Yes, the worst is behind us, we collectively feel. Little does any of us realize as we set out on this last section how trying it will be, how great a toll it will exact from us all.

The temperature drops steadily to below the freezing point as we rise in altitude, the ground growing more rugged by the step. The light mist changes to rain, sleet, then snow. Struggling uphill over the icy ground with their heavy load on the stretcher, the rangers slacken as they tire from the cold, exposure, wind, and exertion. Meanwhile, Odd does his best to coerce and urge them on. It isn't long before tempers flare. For the first time the rangers squabble among themselves, screaming and yelling at one another that they aren't doing their share. The past days' efforts have pushed them to the brink of exhaustion. It's up to Odd now to make sure they don't go over the edge. Taking control loudly and sternly in Swahili, he squelches the bickering; then, softening, he switches to English, admonishing them, repeatedly offering encouragement. He tells them what a tremendous job they are accomplishing, together as a team, "the greatest rescue ever undertaken upon Kilimanjaro." The change in their attitude is sudden and incredible. Odd finds the words and actions, as he has with me, to elicit hidden reserves. The total commitment and respect they give to this man are enviable.

Once we are upon the level, snow-covered Shira Plateau, the going becomes easier. However, radio communication is no longer possible for the rest of the journey, as the mass of Kilimanjaro blocks all signals. The temperature continues to drop. We are exposed to the full force of the snow and the wind as the wind-chill factor dips well below zero. Even protected as I am in the stretcher by my sleeping bag and several waterproof covers, I feel the seeping cold. It shakes my body with violent fits of shivering, deadening my muscles. It is unbearable. Soon the shivers stop, and the unassuming, persuasive desire for sleep creeps over me. I am so tired. Try as I may to shrug it off, the urge grows and takes hold of me. Suddenly my mind recognizes the plight I am in and screams the alarm, "You're freezing to death, do something." Yet the body will not respond; no longer does it follow the will of the mind. I realize now: this is what it is like to freeze to death. I am physically powerless to prevent it. The rocking, jogging gait of the stretcher-laden natives will not even be interrupted by my death. In a moment's time rescuers will become pallbearers, and they won't even know it. I must let Odd know! I can't!

The rescue team soon stops for a rest break under the lee side of a huge umbrellalike boulder that offers protection from the blowing snow. Odd removes the black nylon sheet covering my head, and the driven snow whips across my face, stinging me into consciousness. My eyes desperately search out the orange-clad figures of the rescue team in this torturous world of white. But my mouth utters not a word. It will not work. Only my mind can scream, "Help!"

When Odd asks how I am, he realizes from my numbed inability to reply the severity of my condition. He quickly releases the stretcher straps and vigorously massages my body. The rangers meanwhile huddle around the small gas stove, melting snow for warm water. The infection that riddles my system, the lack of food and water, the binding constriction of the stretcher, all contribute to my deterioration, but especially the cold. After constant massaging and many cups of warm water liberally spiked with glucose powder, I slowly begin to thaw and improve.

With improvement, other needs arise. I must urinate. Immobilized as I am on the stretcher, it is impossible from this position. Odd instructs the rangers to lift the head of the stretcher and hold it vertically upright to make it easier for me. I bear down, straining to piss into the small white porcelain cup Odd holds, the cup from which I have just drunk. I cannot. But I must go. My bladder is about to burst. As a last resort, the stretcher is canted beyond the vertical, so that I am now beneath it. Only the slackened lashing holds me in place, affording any support. Sagging against the constricting bonds, I gasp for every breath. Several minutes of struggling brings no results. Then, just when I have reached my limit, it starts drop by drop and continues, quickly bringing relief. Odd's alarm increases with each splutter. My urine is black as pitch against the side of the white cup, thick and viscous as pine tar. None of us knows why, nor have we the time now to wonder. We must hurry on. Within half an hour I am well enough recovered to continue.

As we approach the far edge of the Shira Plateau, the weather becomes ever more temperate. Finally the sun breaks out of the angry gray sky and bathes us in its warmth. Yet, simultaneously, almost every man in the rescue team fast approaches the limit of his physical endurance. Carriers need to be spelled every hundred yards or so now to rest and to recuperate. Only two rangers, William and Hubert, can still manage longer distances. These two make tremendously fast time by balancing the front and rear of the stretcher on their heads. Moving ahead at a steady jog, they eat up the ground across the moorland, leaving the remainder of the lagging team far behind. It is just after a particularly long carry by these two, taking us off the plateau table down to the final slopes, that Odd notices that two of the youngest rangers have disappeared. During a rest break they must have decided they had had enough, so they ran away and hid. Odd cannot hide his disappointment. The downcast look on his face reveals his hurt. In some way he feels personally responsible for their actions. How would the others react? Mass desertion? The remainder of the team meets the disappearance with somber complacency, pulling and working together all the more to make up for the others' absence.

At last two rectangular specks that our minds tell us are our vehicles come into view. Their size increases with frustrating slowness. When finally we do arrive, the scene looks almost absurd: a battered old green Jeepster and a brand-new Toyota Land Cruiser sit side by side amidst the endless rolling moorlands of wildest Africa. Behind, the brooding hulk of Kilimanjaro dominates the horizon.

The placid scene is soon shattered by an explosive barrage of outbursts in torrid Swahili, announcing the attempted inconspicuous return of our deserters. The two are quickly surrounded and set upon by the remainder of the rangers. The rage and the insults fly at them fast and thick. With tearful eyes downcast, the two remorsefully and silently take their verbal lashing. Although their search for forgiveness and acceptance will go unanswered today, they will not be left behind.

The vehicles quickly loaded, we are soon under way to negotiate the final of our obstacles, three rain-swollen, muddy rivers. Like immense brown cleavers they have gashed great chasms in our path to Moshi and the hospital. Stomping the accelerator to the floorboards, each driver successively launches his vehicle headlong into the brown swirling rapids. He forces the vehicle, grinding, bumping along, across onto the safety of dry land. Then again without interruption he plunges it into the next rushing torrent. Each one of the crossings proves more desperate and severe than the previous. The third and final ford is three feet deep and fifty feet wide. The boiling rapids slam broadside into the Land Cruiser, nudging it sideways downstream. As the driver struggles for control, the water mounds up to the windowpanes in bubbling waves. Fast losing our momentum, we just make it to the far edge of the riverbank and escape.

Once across, Odd turns and assures me how lucky we were today. Many times in the past he has been stranded by this river, unable to cross it for days. Having just experienced our lunge across its uncontrolled fury, I reply weakly that I need no more convincing. I gaze out from the second seat of the Land Cruiser and watch the dying golden sun go blood red as it sinks to the horizon, setting fire to the plains of Africa.

XI

A pill, a needle
Any potion will do
To ease this pain
Make it still

With the deepening gloaming we leave behind the vast rolling moorland and submerge into the forestland. The dark forms of the windblown trees take on sinister shapes in the blackness, swinging their threatening shadows about our heads. The brilliant twin beams of the Land Cruiser keep the specters at bay, casting a ten-by-thirty-foot mat of light ahead of us. Odd, Athanasi, every man sits silent, on edge, alert. Slowly we navigate a winding course ever downward through the towering conifers. As we veer sharply rightward on a tight hairpin turn, a wave of luxurious scent suddenly floods the interior of the Land Cruiser. Although no one else seems to notice, I shout out in surprise, "Oh, smell that! Do you smell that?" It is like the strong, concentrated perfume of lilacs, or is it roses? I do not know. It is not like any scent; then again, it is every scent I ever experienced. I fill my lungs to bursting with the luscious odor. I am overwhelmed with joy; my sense of smell has returned. Who was it that said there is no pleasure like the recovery of the ordinary? He is right. For so many breaths I have inhaled lifeless, barren rock and ice devoid of all olfactory beauty. The smells, sounds, and sights of life were lost from memory, a memory that must fight for its very existence. The senses have cowered before the apparition of death, that ever-present, hideous, rank defile-

193

ment of rotting flesh. This eerie passage through the forest is the return journey to life: the sensuous land of the living.

Hour upon hour we descend the sprawling flanks of the mountain, passing through the various climatic zones. The yellow-green cast of the headlights upon the roadside vegetation offers only a blurred hint of our lowering in altitude. Alpine conifers give way to the mahogany hardwoods of the rain forest, then finally jungle. Yet, as little as we can see of our whereabouts in this ink, one invisible sign is unmistakable. The heat! With every thousand feet we drop in height, the temperature soars upward eight to ten degrees. In the jungle the temperature is over ninety degrees. Even in the shelter of night the heat is oppressive. From earlier in the day, during our journey across the Shira Plateau, to this point, the temperature has risen more than seventy degrees. From every pore a flood of perspiration pours forth over my body. I shed layer upon layer of sweat-soaked clothing for some relief. But it is futile; the interior of the Land Cruiser becomes a sauna. Six sweating bodies create a fog impossible to clear from the windshield.

I crook my head out the right-hand side of the vehicle in search of the slightest cool breeze, but there's nothing; just a moving wall of hot, stifling, moisture-laden air so dense and heavy I fight for every breath. For the first time since the accident I begin to feel physically how bad off I must be. It is as if my vitality is wrung from me with every drop of sweat. Like warm, soft butter my body melts down and spreads out upon the seat. I feel so drained, I cannot hold my head erect. I struggle not to pass out. My body burns with fever, yet violently I shiver. Nausea and cramps rip through my gut like the slashes of knives. Why now after so many days? Suddenly I am deteriorating so quickly. The heat and humidity! On the mountain, the cold and the altitude had kept my infection at bay, dormant. Now in the jungle climate the necrosis has come alive and begins to run rampant. I shudder with the grim thought I'm being devoured, eaten alive from within my own body. My body, ever gracious host, feeds a multitude of microscopic cannibals.

Through the many layers of bandages and dressings covering the wound on my leg there soon filters that rotting stench, my dreaded consort all too familiar these recent days. It saturates the cab of the Cruiser, forcing Odd and the rangers to lean out the windows for relief. An insistent throb pumps through my left leg, reaching up into my groin. It echoes beat for beat the pounding of my heart. Reaching down to my knee to feel the pulse with my fingers, I find the once loose, blousing pant leg of my overtrousers now drawn up taut around my swollen leg. For its full length my leg has ballooned up double its normal size. "Odd," I say as if he does not realize it, "we must get to the hospital soon. Please."

The image of a dimly lit operating room flashes into my mind; there in the amber lamp I imagine the masked surgeon, somber, pensive, brow covered with perspiration. There he stands for several minutes, motionless, staring down at the draped, sleeping patient. He sighs, then grasps the bone saw at his side in his right hand. Precisely aligning the serrated blade over the mid-tibia, he drives it deep into the flesh with several rapid sawing motions. The teeth bite deep. In less than a minute, as skillfully and quickly as an old carpenter dealing with a two-by-four, the surgeon has severed my foot from my leg. "Oh, please, God," I whisper softly, "please don't let this happen now. I've fought too hard for such an ending." Then and there I know that death is preferable. In my vision, I grieve not so much for the loss of my foot as for what it symbolizes. A one-footed alpinist! I lament the loss of my life's loves, mountains and climbing. Footless, bound for the rest of my days as a prisoner in the valley, I would see the beauty and grandeur of the peaks high above, feel their lure, yet never again enter their midst. Hearing the continual enticement of their soft siren song would soon drive me mad, knowing that never again could I succumb to it. I'd be better dead.

Still I await the final verdict. Within me writhe the worms of anguish, gnawing at my stomach. The days of waiting, the unknowns eat away at me as surely as does the infection.

Before long we arrive at the Shira Forestry gate, the end of the spreading skirts of Kilimanjaro and the start of the valley floor. We head off left down the paved highway toward Moshi Town. On the smooth surface the Land Cruiser is soon streaking through the night at nearly fifty miles an hour, bringing us all fresh air and welcome relief—but my leg continues to worsen. My trousers stretch like the skin of a balloon inflated by the continued swelling. So, too, does my anxiety. The slightest movement, the mere tensing of my thigh muscles to hold my position in the shifting vehicle, brings spasms of agony.

Within the hour we arrive at the outskirts of Moshi Town, mere bamboo shanties rising amidst the overpowering jungle growth. Even this simple sign of civilization cheers me. "It is not long now, Rob," Odd reassures me over his shoulder from the front seat. "We shall be there in just some minutes now." Approaching a dimly lit, unmarked intersection, our driver barrels straight on through at a steady fifty miles per hour. Midway through the intersection, the left side of our Land Cruiser is suddenly ablaze with light. Intently peering out the side window, I watch the illuminated metallic grill of the other vehicle swell in size and detail. I can see the battered lettering, PE G . . . a Peugeot. In an instant it is going to hit us right behind the second door. Sucking back a gasp, I brace myself for the crash. The Peugeot, entering the intersection a scant second after us or perhaps traveling a split second slower, misses us by inches. Neither driver hesitates or reacts; neither allows the other a trace of recognition. It happens so quickly, there is no time to be frightened. But, recovering from my shock, I can imagine the grisly state of this vehicle and its mangled occupants if we had been a second slower. My mind can visualize the news copy:

TANZANIA: Gravely injured American mountain climber killed today in freak car accident on way to hospital after surviving five days on Mt. Kilimanjaro.

There is such irony to it. The human spirit possesses an awesome strength of will, allowing man to endure the harshest of extremes and suffering interminably. Yet, in the end, the declicate frailty of the human body hinges on the whims of fate.

Under the cover of darkness, Thursday begins to exhale its last breath, about to lose the battle of time to Friday. Shortly Odd motions with a jab of a finger for the driver to brake and pull over to some unseen spot in the darkness. There, as if sprouted from the plants that entwine it, stands a classic English Victorian phone booth, even painted red.

Odd opens the door of the Cruiser, bathing the interior with pale-yellow light. "Rob, I shall call Dr. Moirer," he states. "He is a friend of mine and will treat you. I must telephone him now to have him meet us at KCMC." KCMC is the Kilimanjaro Christian Medical Center at Moshi. Several minutes elapse and he returns. "There is no answer at his house," he softly says, as much to himself as to me, in puzzlement. "Nor is he at the hospital; I don't know, Rob," he adds, "I have also called my home in Marangu; neither my wife, Rotraut, nor Harley are there, either." A few final seconds' contemplation, and he jumps back into the Land Cruiser. "Ah, perhaps they shall meet us at the hospital." Off we roar.

Entering into the confines of the KCMC Hospital compound, we momentarily stop at Dr. Moirer's cottage, directly adjacent to the hospital buildings. "Perhaps he has come home now," Odd states as he jumps from the Land Cruiser. A quick exchange in front of the house with a shadowy figure, Dr. Moirer's wife, and Odd hurriedly returns. "Dr. Moirer is not here, he has been called out into the bush on an emergency. Don't worry, it's OK, there is another good doctor awaiting us at the hospital. Let's go."

A drive of two-hundred yards and we are there. In the darkness my eyes are drawn and locked onto the yellow glow of the sulfur lamps marking the entrance.

Odd and Athanasi help ease me from the vehicle and try to hold me upright as my eyes fill with a streaking, dazzling brilliance of a hundred stabs of white light. The ringing of bells in my ears blots out all other sounds. The rangers catch me as I double over. For the final steps into the hospital Odd and

Athanasi firmly grasp my arms over their shoulders. My attempt at hops are mere dragged scrapes upon the ground.

There are no doors separating the inside of the hospital from the outside. The only delineation is where darkness succumbs to light, where lush vegetation gives way to grimy gray-tiled walls seamed with dirt.

In the vestibule I collapse onto a decrepit wooden gurney covered with a soiled green surgical sheet. Like water seeking its own level, my body oozes down onto its right side into a semiprostrate position. I've made it. What a great release I feel. From within erupts a long sighing exhalation. Yet there is something about this place that puts me on edge, an apprehension that rattles within. Staring upward at the green, cracked, paint-blistered ceiling, I watch several immense cream-colored moths circle and dance wildly about the exposed bulb overhead. No more easily can I explain this apprehension than why these moths so dashingly flirt with death. Perhaps they are driven to the light by much the same fatal attraction that draws the alpinist to his death in the mountains.

Odd takes a quick look about the hospital in search of Rotraut and Harley. Returning, he says, "Rob, I don't understand it; they're not here, and I tried the phone again, no answer at home still. Where can they be?"

Lying on the table, I am enveloped by a fatigue that goes almost beyond caring. A fatal fatigue that softly and enticingly murmurs: Come to sleep, come, be left alone to rest—forever. It is irresistible. So desirable!

"Dr. Isaakson," says Odd, seeing a figure fast approaching, drawing me from my somnolence.

He is a tall, painfully thin man, balding, with glasses, so slightly built that his hospital garb appears to droop from his meager frame as if hung from coat hangers. In slightly accented English he speaks in a voice barely above a whisper. Slowly he puts forth each word to give it the necessary emphasis, hesitatingly, as if he were duly considering each for its meaning.

With every completed sentence he pauses intermittently, gazing out into space, seemingly lost in deep thought, then startlingly continues on. With our introductions I learn that he is Swedish. A surgeon who has been doing missionary work in Africa for some seven years. At my side Odd and he converse for several minutes in their native tongues, he in Swedish and Odd in Norwegian. I am surprised they can communicate so easily in languages sounding so different to me. Then Dr. Isaakson retreats down the hall.

What are these two doing here in Africa? Scandinavia is such a beautiful land. What could ever compel a man to give it up in exchange for this? After so many years of myths and rumors, perhaps it is true—perhaps there do exist Dr. Albert Schweitzers, blessed, merciful souls committed to the lifelong service of man.

In a moment the doctor returns, clutching a large gleaming scalpel and a pair of forceps in his right hand. Leaning over my left ankle, he deftly begins sawing away at the bulky mound of bandages covering it. Within me, that almost exhausted trickle of adrenalin suddenly gushes forth its all, releasing into my system its last reserves. I come to life; fear and anxiety flood my every pore. Bandages that hide . . . ? With each passing second my pulse mounts. In only minutes I shall know the final verdict. Please, Jesus, please let my foot be alive. Dr. Isaakson slowly severs and neatly pulls aside layer upon layer. The waiting. The uncertainty. Beneath these final shreds of cloth, hidden from my eyes, lies my future.

I squirm back on the table with every draw of the scalpel as I imagine it slicing into my own flesh. Flesh once vital, alive and pink, now. . . ? Firmly, Dr. Isaakson steadies my leg, pinning it in place on the gurney with his elbow and free hand, enlisting Odd to help him. The nearer he approaches the wound, the more discolored and sodden the dressing becomes. Please, God, don't let it be too late. I can resist no longer; nervously I ask, "Dr. Isaakson, what do you think?" There is no response from him, not even a nod of the head or a glance of the eyes acknowledging my question. Does that mean it is too late, that all is lost? I try to convince myself that this is not the case, that he would know nothing until the wound is totally exposed.

The final double sheaths of cotton gauze are brilliant yellow-green, flecked with pink and red, so wet and saturated with pus they are partially decomposed. As Dr. Isaakson tries to remove them they disintegrate. Ever so gently he must dislodge piece by piece of the matter from the wound with the tip of the scalpel. It is a slow, tedious process. At last he mutters, "There!"

Within me the dam bursts; I pour forth a tirade of questions that deny the seriousness of my predicament. "How does it look, Doctor? Is it OK? If it is OK and it is acceptable to you, I would prefer going to the United Kingdom for treatment. I even have a friend who will escort me on the trip." His gaze firmly fixed on the wound, Dr. Isaakson makes no reply.

Lying there on my back, I cannot see the foot clearly. The many layers of my clothing rolled up upon my leg obscure my view. Odd, joining Dr. Isaakson, looks down at the wound. He manages only a startled "Ohwa!" as the blood drains from his face. "I don't believe it," he says. "It's so much worse now!" I search Dr. Isaakson's face for some hint of a reaction: the creasing of his forehead, the tightening of his lips, or perhaps the narrowing of his eyes, but there is nothing. Not a crack of emotion erodes his staid, granitic expression. Finally he answers, "I am afraid leaving for treatment is impossible."

I must see it for myself. Leaning forward, I rise above the bundled clothing. It is a sight I do not want to look at. I feel I must. To know, once and for all. My eyes trace the lines of my lower leg. It is so bloated, so distended, there is no form to it any longer, just a mass of ashen-gray skin stretched so taut it is translucent, glistening. Downward the swelling increases and the color deepens. My foot and ankle area are unrecognizable—a tumescent blob of purple and black, larger than a football, a revolting sight, yet I cannot look away. I must know it all. I crane my neck forward to examine the wound on the outside of my ankle. The withered skin marking the edges of the wound is caked thick and black with dry blood. The center is a pool of green liquid dribbling onto the discarded dressing. The remaining surface of the wound is covered by a latticework of cobweblike filaments of coagulated yellow pus. Beneath the upper edge of the wound I see the off-white bulging round end of the fibula, poking out at me. It is not a pleasant sight, nor a hopeful one. Yet, sitting there upon that creaking gurney, I stare down at it a long while, unflinching, examining its every detail, not a bit queasy or squeamish. No longer is it *my* shattered, rotting leg. Mentally I have become detached from it. It is simply *a* shattered, rotten leg, another of the many hundreds of casualties I have witnessed during my years on the hills in mountain rescue. I feel a deep sadness, recalling its earlier state, so supple, so nimble—gone forever.

"That's it, then," I say, perhaps even a bit relieved. In my work I found that survival is a matter of cold calculation; it is the ultimate reality one faces in this world, demanding clear, honest thinking and positive action. Unrestrained emotions and unbridled feelings in the end, after the fact, are fine, but during the crisis they are illusory defenders. Emotions carry no weight in the realm where Death reigns supreme as a heartless king. Now, for me, the days of waiting, of uncertainty, are over. There are no more unresolved questions. The fear and anxiety dissipate within me. Reality stands before me, the reality of this leg, of this life. Today, for me, there are no alternatives, no choices, no chance procrastinations, no miraculous reversals. Nowhere to run, nowhere to hide. One must stand and face it. I am prepared for the worst and shall accept it.

Dr. Isaakson directs his attention to me, having duly surveyed my ankle for some minutes. "When have you eaten last?" he says. "You are in need of immediate emergency surgery to save your leg perhaps." His voice trails off. "I shall perform a surgical toilet this evening upon your ankle, a debridement exposing the joint interior and to determine the extent of the damage. But first let us take some X rays." He grabs the front of the gurney, and, with Odd on the rear, we head off from the lighted entrance into the darkness. The eerie unlit corridor is deserted, silent, save for the shuddering of the gurney wheels over the curling linoleum tiles and an indistinguishable, muffled sound like moaning. It resounds throughout the corridor, on and on. The signs on all doors and hallways are printed in white boldface Swahili with the English equivalent below in smaller letters: UTABIBU, WAL-IOZIDIWA, UPASUAJI, WAUGUZI. The Swahili words flash by, alien, each looking very much like the other, full of Zs, Us, and Ws. I struggle to catch their English counterparts. The contrast is puzzling, when I think of a simple language like Swahili trying to represent such technical, complex scientific terms as immunology, bacteriology, pathology.

I am bewildered upon entering the X-ray room: it is as full of futuristic and sophisticated equipment as any I have seen in the United States or Britain. Closer inspection in the dim light reveals to me, however, quite a different countenance. It is in a terrible state: full of dents, gouges, and scratches, having suffered a lifetime of knocks and abuse. Who could do this? What kind of assailants? A small metallic placard upon the control panel provides me with an explanation: This most generous gift to the peoples of Tanzania is from an enlightened and benevolent nation. Perhaps it is Germany, the United Kingdom, Russia, or China. It matters little. It is foreign aid. A form of aid that from the looks of things is little understood and even less respected by Tanzanians. I wonder if perhaps the peoples of Tanzania would not have more appreciated a different form of aid, something more meaningful, more identifiable to them. I can well imagine that X-ray film goes down very poorly on an empty stomach. I soon see that anomalies such as this—a delicate, complex piece of space-age machinery sitting in the midst of the jungles of Africa, amidst a people fighting the ravages of hunger, cholera and pellagra—are typical of the awesome contrasts of Africa.

X rays taken, Dr. Isaakson shortly reappears from within the depths of the developing room. At the side of the gurney he says to me, "You do not have a fracture of the fibula as suspected. The bone was grossly dislocated in your fall, exposing your ankle joint. You do, however, show a comminuted fracture of the talus. And the rampant infection you exhibit is very grave, demanding immediate and utmost attention. At once I shall arrange for surgery; you shall be taken to be prepared for the operation." The days alone weigh on my memory as I realize the time the infection has had to grow. If only I had been rescued earlier.

Odd moves the gurney with me on it back into the corridor. Here in the darkness an apparition seemingly suspended in space glides toward us, zeroing in on Dr. Isaakson. Soft whispers are exchanged in Swahili. Then there is resolve and silence as they part company. Dr. Isaakson turns and slips into the shadows away from us, while the ghostly apparition grasps the front of the gurney and slowly begins plodding back toward the entrance, gurney in tow. I peer toward the figure, straining to catch some outline of his features, a facial expression or even an eye glint. Yet there is nothing revealed in this darkness. Once I am returned to the light of the vestibule, my apparition's true identity is finally revealed to me. He's a thickset Bantu orderly with a round, cheery face, his glistening skin as black and shiny as the finest polished ebony. As the orderly draws the gurney across the lobby floor, Odd, on the rear and silent all this time, speaks to me.

"Rob! They are still not here. I must try Rotraut again."

"Sure, Odd," I say to the empty space above me as he leaves to try the phone once more.

The orderly meanwhile draws the gurney leftward into a side room, and then, within the room, into a small cloth-partitioned cubicle.

"Mista," he says, as I look up to meet his gaze, "dasista wull took care a yoo hair sun. Ock-key? Hum Damien, say u sun."

"Yeah, sure," I answer, staring into his white-and-murky-

brown eyes, not sure at all what he has said. These pupilless eyes
enrobed in a thick film of yellow mucus hold no hint for me. He
turns and retreats. I suspect this room to be the pre-op, as it reeks
of that antiseptic smell so familiar in hospitals and doctors'
offices, almost like a cross between formaldehyde and alcohol, a
smell that every time prickles the hair on my neck, setting me on
edge. I am anxious now to get this inevitable thing under way,
that it can be finished. It has been enough days, enough waiting.

As I crane my head around the pleated cloth barrier, my eyes
scan the room for someone, anyone. A long counter opposite me
runs the length of the room, lined with canister upon canister of
cotton gauze and bandages. Before them, haphazardly strewn
about, lie trays of disorganized instruments and beside these a
myriad of brown glass bottles of all shapes and sizes, seemingly
unlabeled. Stretching leftward on the gurney, I continue my
visual search down the counter. At first I see nothing extraordin-
ary, only more disarray upon the counter. Then I see a small
sliver of navy-blue cloth, like a uniform. It is just out of sight
beyond the barricade. What could that be? My curiosity whet-
ted, I press myself flat against the gurney top and shift my weight
about to nudge it forward a few inches and get a better look. A
few of these maneuvers and I can see easily around the barricade.
There in the corner at the end of the room sits a smallish black
woman dressed in a navy-blue uniform, a navy-blue cape
fastened over her shoulders and a white nurse's cap upon her
head. She slouches over the counter, balancing in a decrepit
wooden chair whose left front leg is at least one and a half inches
shorter than the others. Head resting in her open right palm,
supported in turn by her elbow resting on the counter top, she is
just on the verge of sleep. Stealthily, drowsiness finally over-
comes her; she nods off to a quiet snore. Within seconds, her
body relaxes, and the chair comes crashing forward, instantly
jolting her out of her slumber. She casts a groggy eye about.
Then she settles back into her former position, only to duplicate
this procedure once more: becoming sleepy, nodding off, shunted

awake by the crashing chair, gazing about, then settling back in. I watch enthralled as she repeats this same cycle time again.

"Rob!" The soft calls of Odd snap me from my trance.

"Here, Odd!" I answer as he enters the pre-op room.

"Ah! There!" he says, "I have finally reached Rotraut. She is home."

"Good, that's a relief, anyway." Yet his somber face, forehead creased in introspective puzzlement, reflects anything but relief. The unusually strained tenseness in his voice makes me suspect that something is amiss. "Odd," I ask, "is anything wrong? Everything OK?" Looking up, instantly I see the darkness sweep from his face, submerging within him.

"Oh! . . . Ah! . . . Ah! . . . Yah! Fine! Good! It's just they were here waiting for us for some time. We must have missed them."

"Oh!" I say, my voice trailing off, leaving an empty, uneasy silence between us. Although he looks quite normal now, that inflection, that nervousness in his voice, still persists. It is unsettling. Perhaps it is simply a matter of exhaustion catching up with him after so many days.

"Rob," Odd says, "I must go now to get some food and sleep. Dr. Isaakson will take care of you. There is nothing more tonight I can do for you."

"Sure, Odd," I say. "Thanks very much for all you've done."

"See you tomorrow morning," he says. He turns to go.

At the doorway I call out to him, "Odd, please make sure Harley comes as soon as possible. OK?"

"Ah! . . . Ah!" His face flushes once more. "OK, Rob. I'll take care of it. See you tomorrow." He whirls around, disappearing out the doorway, but his troubled visage stays etched into my mind.

An icy uneasiness wraps its unseen fingers around my body. It sends a cold shiver up my back. Simultaneously I break out in goose bumps and a heavy sweat. I lie on the gurney, alone with my thoughts, the room silent, save for the nurse's repetitive, clockwork, chair-rocking cycle. Try as I may I cannot forget that look upon Odd's face nor what it might mean.

Time passes. An hour. Two hours. My scratched Timex marks the time all too slowly. No one ever comes, nothing happens. There is only this hellish waiting. As I lie on the gurney, finally I fall asleep, dreaming. I have escaped Africa and its pains. It can do me no harm now.

I am whole once more, roaming free, climbing upon the legion of precipitous mountain walls of my imagination. Big Ben, Mount Desolation, Mount Analog. Effortlessly I surmount every obstacle they present, the smooth arching wall of granite, the razor-thin knife-edge arête, the vertical barrier of rotten snow seracs waiting to avalanche. All difficulties melt away and fall below me as I drift upward. As if soaring, I ascend onward to their pristine summits, bootless, unclothed, completely unencumbered by the necessities of alpine safety and survival. I am impervious to the mortal dangers mountains pose to men now. I am at one with them.

In the early-morning hours of Friday, the twentieth, I am awakened by a shuffling sound. Opening my eyes, I am disoriented. The fanciful illusions dissipate in the heat and the grimy surroundings I see before me. It comes back to me now. Ah, yes, the pre-op. I check the time: 3:34 A.M. The scuffing shuffling draws my eyes up from my watch and over to the right. The sleepy rocking-chair nurse approaches. Somehow she has roused herself out of her deep torpor and come to life. Puffy-eyed and groggy, she scrapes each foot forward over the linoleum, allowing not the slightest separation between her shoe soles and the surface of the floor. Her slow, skating gait makes her appear frozen in motion as in a TV slo-mo instant replay. Finally, sidling up to my gurney, she leans her full weight against it, as if trying to recover from some great expenditure of energy. Without so much as a word she methodically and mechanically begins stripping off my remaining clothes. She removes them sluggishly, cheerlessly, heaving them in great lumps to the floor. Her face is sallow. Her eyes are murky brown, empty. She moves on to my lower body, and surveys my injured leg with a yawn. Her sleepy boredom, however, soon changes to displeasure, even contempt, when she realizes she must remove my overtrousers, fur pants, and angora underwear over this leg, this leg so much an impediment and inconvenience to her now. Grabbing a fistful of gauze from one of the glass receptacles on the counter, she nonchalantly shoves the wad into my weeping wound. "Yeeowh!" I cry out as a sudden, burning shot of pain explodes within me. I continue to writhe as she firmly presses the wad down while twisting it to stick it securely to the mucus in the wound. I try to escape her torment by skidding backward on the gurney, but she blocks off retreat and escape. Clamping her right hand down securely on the middle toe of my injured leg, she draws it and me back toward her. I am powerless but to submit and endure this torture. Once returned to a comfortable distance from her, I am given a few minutes' respite. I lie back exhausted, then look down over my body to my feet, where she stands. That sleepy, vacant expression is gone now, replaced by a childish grin. She has come alive. I see before me an intimidating, sinister face, filled with amusement. The very sight of it terrifies me. How can a mere look frighten a man used to confronting the danger of mountain walls? Perhaps it is a kind of terror that only human beings can instill, because only humans possess the willfullness and maliciousness to inflict pain upon one another. In my years in the mountains I often saw nature act in catastrophic ways, yet never did it act willfully.

Nervously I watch this nurse reach down to my injured leg once more. She grasps my middle toe between her left thumb and index finger and squeezes it tightly until it hurts. The next few minutes are a distorted blur of agony. My eyes are set ablaze with white shooting stars as she yanks my toe upward. My screams echo in the halls as she lifts my leg off the gurney. My insistent pleas for mercy are intermingled with her heavy, raucous giggling. Suspending my leg solely by that single toe, unsupported in space, she rips the three layers of clothing down from the knee, over the wound and off my foot onto the floor in one fell swoop, allowing my leg to smash back onto the gurney. Still laughing, she turns, shuffling away at a pace fast in contrast to before, but still slow, down the counter into the room. The throbs of pain still vibrating, I lie on the table drained, spent. Please, God, let it be finished. Don't let her re— The telltale scraping scuffling resumes once more before I have even finished my petition to Providence. Into sight she slowly approaches, once more her somber face but a blank, featureless expanse. In one hand she grasps a brown glass flask, in the other a great wad of cotton gauze. At the foot of the gurney she whisks the now pus-saturated coverlet from my wound and indifferently tosses it to the floor. Her careless release of the wet, dripping projectile allows it to fall too close to her body. It smears an inch-wide swath of green slime down the side of her navy-blue skirt before splattering, a direct hit, upon her open-toed leather sandal. Seemingly impervious to the putrid discharge, she dislodges the sodden mass from the top of her foot with a swift short kick, sending it cartwheeling in blotchy, moist patches across the floor out of sight. Uncorking the bottle with her mouth, she pours out a long slender stream of yellow antiseptic-smelling liquid into the new, unused gauze she holds. I brace for the burning sting of the antiseptic as she starts dabbing my leg. But there is none. Only the cold tingling of the liquid on my skin. Evidently finding this method too time- or energy-consuming, she stops after several passes down my leg. Grasping my middle toe once more, she hoists my leg up in space. She holds the flask above my suspended leg, tipping it end over top, and releases its entire contents in one glugging flood upon me. The icy deluge flows first over my foot, then my ankle, leg, lower body. Just as the yellow tide licks at my navel, the bottle empties. After she drops my leg back to the sopping gurney, this "nurse" turns and shuffles out of the room, still giggling under her breath. I lie motionless several minutes until the waves of pain begin to subside in my leg. Yet I am not all that convinced she will not return again to resume her work.

It is a pitiful sight—looking down over this filthy, naked body of mine, awash in a yellow sea of pain and misery. In silence the minutes pass. Within me a record begins to play. The needle sticks on a new refrain: I am alone, helpless, in this alien realm—a forsaken world in which I have no proxy, no control over my own fate. Others, those unknown faces, they will decide and seal my destiny, perhaps forever. Up until the hospital, as desperate as my plight may have been, I felt some control, some power over my fate, even if it meant no more than hopping or crawling down the mountainside. Now I am powerless, and every nurse, every orderly, every doctor, is a potential enemy as well as a potential ally. After so many days fighting, still my spirit must struggle to survive. This spirit, protected by the shell I see before me, is my only companion now, and it is powerless against this enemy, an enemy more formidable than death itself, and one I fear more.

Damien, the Bantu orderly who first brought me to the pre-op, reappears in the doorway. Grinning broadly, he enters the room and grasps the end of the gurney. "Tym-ah-nu, Mistarob," he says, wheeling it out of the room. I know it is time for surgery, although I really do not understand what he says. In his voice there is a warmth and in his actions a sincerity that are so different from the nurse who has dealt with me earlier this night. Somehow I feel I can trust him. Hope flickers within me. Across the brilliantly lighted entrance he pulls me, then down into a dark, unlit corridor, wheels thumping along in the blackness. The flutter of nervousness squirms within me, the anxious anticipation of the immediately impending surgery. Yet I also feel relief. The waiting is finished. While it is still in motion, the orderly adroitly shifts his position on the gurney from the foot to the head and rams it forward through the double swinging doors of the surgical unit. Midway through, he deftly catches both of the rebounding doors with his elbows before they can smash into the gurney. He does care! Here in the small, dim anteroom of the operating room serving both as a surgical prep and as a post-op, the orderly hands me over to two surgically garbed Bantu nurses completely swathed in white except for their eyes and hands. Through the final set of swinging doors they ease the gurney into the O.R. The sickening, sweetish smell of antiseptic is as strong as it was in the pre-op room, but here it is intermingled with, overshadowed by, another ghastly odor, the gagging fetor of blood gone rancid. It smothers me like a heavy blanket as I enter.

Sucking in quick, short gasps of air, I try to escape its foul scent, but it is impossible. The operating room lies in complete blackness save for the single bright beam of the operating lamp illuminating the center. There in the glow of its white shine, so brilliantly white it hurts one's eyes to look at it, lies the table. It is covered by a dark surgical cloth that once must have been green. Now it is forever discolored by countless stains of blood, red blotches that have transformed it into an almost batik pattern. Through the beam of light I see the tall, thin figure of Dr. Isaakson, in surgical green trousers and a stained, sweat-soaked undershirt. He stands in the shadows just on the edge of darkness, his legs and torso illuminated by the light, his neck and head thrust upward, unseen, into the darkness, silent and unmoving. The room vibrates with a faint but constant low-frequency hum that surrounds me but which I cannot locate. The nurses wheel me into the glaring arc of the lamp and prepare to transfer me from the gurney to the table. Flat on my back, eyes dazzled and blinded by the light, I look up past it for relief toward the ceiling into the darkness. There I can see that the room is full of countless small black objects, buzzing to and fro, darting here and there. It's impossible. This operating room is full of bugs! How can a surgical operating room conceivably be allowed to house such an entourage of every kind of crawling and flying insect imaginable?

As I am slid onto the table, the encrusted ridges of dried blood snag at my flesh, digging into my back. I recoil at every touch. Fear and revulsion overwhelm me. "Jesus," I pray, "please deliver me from this living hell!" Dr. Isaakson's head enters the field of light as he approaches me on the right-hand side of the table. "We shall anesthetize you now with sodium Pentothal. When you feel the jab of the injection, count back slowly from one hundred." Across the table from him, my left arm is suddenly grasped and forcibly pulled away from my body. Momentarily I resist as I switch my glance leftward from Dr. Isaakson to this unseen adversary. But I quickly relax when I hear the soft, gentle voice, "Hitokie, Mistarob, down wurri!" Looking up against the glare of the lights, I at first see only a masked face, then those familiar yellowish eyes appear to me. It is Damien, the man who I assumed was an orderly, but who now, in fact, is the anesthesiologist. It is reassuring that he is here, but even so I feel alone, unprotected.

After tying the tourniquet tightly around my upper arm, Damien's fingers search out an easy entrance for the drug. I jump slightly with the jab of the needle and relax my muscles. Instantly I feel the shimmering ripple of the narcotic lap against the shores of my mind. Gazing upward, directly into the blinding light of the surgical lamp, I see it once more, the great white hulking dome of Kilimanjaro, brilliant, shimmering in the sun. On all sides combers surround me. I know now this is where I am going. Back to Kilimanjaro, back to the Breach Wall. Suddenly a great wave breaks over me, like the swell of a pounding Pacific breaker. I am awash, struggling in its swirling wake. The undertow claws at me, pulling me down. "No!" In an instant I am subm . . .

XII

Two to Africa
One remains
It's hard to resist
The call of fame

"Rob! Rob!" The noise intrudes upon my realm of purest whiteness. Once more it softly sounds. "Rob! Rob!" Listlessly adrift in this nebulous domain, my eyes, my mind, my mind's eyes search for the noise.

Sometime later, the shrouds of mist enveloping me slowly begin to dissipate. The heat. It is so hot. It blows over me like the fire of a furnace. This fire now swarms downward, centralizing itself at one point in my lower body, my leg.

Suddenly a blur of colors dances before my eyes. I hear once more "Rob? Rob?" A few seconds more. Multiple crossed images focus into vision. I see at the foot of the bed Odd and a dark-haired woman staring down at me. "Rob, how are you? This is my wife, Rotraut."

I answer him with only an "Oh, no!" as what I hoped was a bad dream focuses back into reality.

Odd repeats, "Rob, how are you?"

Suddenly I remember my foot, and lift my head weakly off the pillow, feebly pushing myself forward. I must know if I still have it.

"Rob, it's OK," Odd says to me, just as I get my first glimpse of it.

It's true! I still have my foot. It swings before me strapped securely onto a narrow cotton stretcher board pulled into traction above me, yet still I am not prepared for the sight of it. The toes, swollen, purple-hued, hang like a bunch of Pinot Noir grapes, frozen in place, immovable, try as I may to wiggle them. The ankle, its running wound now a gaping hole, greatly enlarged and deeply excavated, sprouts long red rubber surgical hoses. With my eyes I trace their paths down from the huge gallon IV bottle suspended above my bed. One enters the center of the wound on the outside of my ankle and erupts out on the opposite, inner side of my ankle joint. The other pierces my instep through an incision and gouges vertically down through my ankle joint, boring out just right of my heel. What have they done to me? The ends of the two hoses hang limply in space, disgorging a steady flow of brown pus. The droplets exit the tubes and, splutter upon splutter, fall into the rectangular metal basin resting beside me on the bed. Searing pain radiates from my distended toes up through the lymph nodes in my groin, consuming my entire body with its burning throb. Yet this pervasive ache is a constant reminder, an assurance I am still whole.

As I see Odd and Rotraut there, it suddenly hits me. "Where's Harley?" They turn to each other with clouded, troubled faces. "Is he all right? Has something happened to him?" Still no response.

I look to Rotraut's warm brown eyes. They retreat into a watery pool. Still avoiding my gaze, she breaks the silence, "Ah . . . Rob . . . Harley's gone. He's left."

I am dumbstruck, dazed. My mouth forms the words in disbelief, "Harley's gone? He's left?" But I am unable to utter them aloud.

My ears ring once more with Harley's last words to me, there in the falling snow beneath the great tumbling headwall of the Heim Glacier. "OK, Rob, I'm off—be back late tonight or very early tomorrow morning with the rescue party. . . . Take it easy—rest, the worst is over now. I'm gonna take care of everything, so don't worry. . . . We've made it this far; we'll make it all the way." Across the mounded pumice moraines mottled with white, I watch Harley's blue-clad figure slowly vanish into the curtain of heavily falling snow.

Out of sight. Out of Africa . . .

"Rob! Please," Rotraut continues. "Harley wanted to see you . . . he waited for you . . . but it got late . . . you didn't arrive . . . he would have missed his flight . . . he said he had to leave . . . he had to get back . . . he had most important business . . . he couldn't afford to miss it . . . I am sorry!"

Involuntarily my eyes fill. "How could Harley have left without seeing me, without even knowing if I'd make it?"

"Rob," Odd says, "I'm sorry. Rotraut told me on the phone last night. But I couldn't tell you, not then. You see, Rob, Harley told Rotraut that he had to leave. She couldn't make him stay."

On and on they speak to me, trying their best to comfort and hearten me, but I hear none of it. Their voices dissolve into an incessant droning in my ears.

I retreat within. Thoughts out of the past return now to haunt me: a very special kinship between two climbers . . . bonded into a union . . . each having absolute faith, reliance and responsibility . . . two become one, think as one, joined in the brotherhood of the rope, their unbreakable lifeline. . . .

"Rob!" says Odd, forcing his presence back into my consciousness, "we must go now."

"We will return later, when you feel better," adds Rotraut.

I acknowledge their departure with a limp shake of the head, then resubmerge into myself.

Why? Over and over again meanings for his actions churn in my mind. Friendship with Harley? Was I expecting too much? I never did consider us friends, so why should I now presume upon the benefits of friendship?

But what about the brotherhood of the rope? I felt we had a commitment to each other that went beyond friendship. Even if he stayed only to see me through until death. If our roles were reversed, never would I leave Africa before he was able to. Much less without seeing him, without knowing if he would survive. Rotraut said, "Harley had to go." What emergency could have demanded this? Originally he scheduled his departure for the nineteenth to attend a sports convention in Houston. That can't be why he left!

I keep wanting to explain his absence, to find a convenient, logical shelf in my mind to put it on. But the puzzlement—the anger at him for not being here to help me—clouds my consciousness.

I must put Harley out of mind. Time will explain all.

Days pass. . . . How many days is it? Another operation. I am too sick with fever and infection to notice. My soaked straw mattress is alive with the buzzing and rustling of countless fleas and lice. I glance around the surgical ward for the first time. There are seven beds besides my own, crammed into a fifteen-by-twenty-five-foot yellow-cast room. All of them are filled. The outer wall of the ward is a screened expanse with wooden blinds dividing the interior of the hospital from the outdoors. Through the open slats the thick, luxurious jungle vegetation bears down threateningly upon the hospital as if any second it will overwhelm it. The menacing tangle of branches and leaves obscures all sights but one. Upward, past the topmost fronds of the palms, the western flank of Kilimanjaro rises to its great squarish dome of snow, glistening in the sun. Within the room there is no noise, no movement from the other beds, only the sound of the rhythmic, labored breathing gently heaving in and out, in and out, in the humid searing heat.

To my left, next to the window, his back to me, lies a smallish, squat black man. At one and the same time he is very stocky yet extraordinarily thin. Across his wide shoulders and thick back each rib bone and every vertebra of the spine stand out clearly under tautly stretched skin. Midway down his back, just an inch to the right of his spine, there is a hole out of which exits a large clear plastic tube swirling down into a gallon-size glass jar beneath his bed. Drip by drip a brown liquid flows through the coil into the already half-full jar on the floor. Across the room from him, right next to the window, lies another man face down, entirely entombed in white plaster. Only his palms, the soles of his feet, and a small black square patch over his buttocks are exposed. In the bed next to his the small rounded form of a child lies huddled beneath a sheet. Where the lines of the sheet and the straw pillow merge, I can just make out his tiny face, eyes closed, apparently asleep. His head is obscured by bloodied bandages. Blotch upon red blotch saturates the dressings like painted red carnations from just above his left ear, continuing across his forehead to above his right eye. Next to him there lies an ancient Masai tribesman. I cannot mistake him. The Masai are a tribe unique in appearance, tall, whiplike, aristocratic. Hoary and grizzled with age, he stares out into space. His tall slender body has long since withered to bones and skin. Yet he retains his stature and bears it proudly. Flat on his back, he is naked except for a small brown loincloth. His right knee, pulled upward above him in traction, is suspended from two pins, one running through his knee joint and the other through his ankle.

The bed on the other side of the Masai is beyond my line of sight, yet, lifting my head slightly forward, I see a plaster-covered arm and two legs also encased in plaster, thrust upward in traction. Of the patient across from him on my side of the room I can see nothing. He is totally blocked from my view by the man in the bed next to me. This fellow, propped on his pillow, is the liveliest of the lot. He sits, faded red fez tilted forward on his head and framing his small face, totally absorbed in a missallike book. There are definite differences between him and the others. Although he is as old, thin and withered as the Masai, his coal-black skin as dark as that of the rest of the Africans in the room, he is smaller, much smaller and slighter, than any of them. His features, especially his nose, brow, and chin, are very sharp and angular, more akin to those of an Arab than of any black man I have ever seen. He looks up from his reading and smiles at me, simultaneously closing his eyes, nodding his head gently forward toward me in silent greeting. Sheepishly I return the gesture to him. As I settle back once more to rest he returns to his prayer book.

I was told Kilimanjaro Christian Medical Center is one of the finest hospitals—by African standards—yet it is grossly different from my Western conception of a hospital. At times the respect and treatment given the human body concurred more with the atmosphere of a morgue than of a medical center.

In the heat the throbbing in my leg continues, the smell of rotting flesh filling the ward. The rectangular discharge can on my bed, long since filled to overflowing, spills its slimy pus-laden contents about my buttocks and lower back.

Escape. . . . I succumb to the beguiling summons of slumber.

"Where am I? I don't know this place." Before me there rises a sheer fang of ice. For thousands of feet it soars upward, slicing into the heavens of eternal night. Its smooth vertiginous surface is perfect, unblemished, shining deep blue in the eerie light. Someone else is here.

"Who's there?"

"Rob?"

"Harley!"

"Yes!"

"At last. I've found you. We became separated."

"I know, somehow we lost each other!"

"Yes, but it's over now. We're reunited."

Together again as partners we shall tackle this mountain face before us. Crampons and ice axes blazing a trail of pinpricks upon its mirrorlike finish, we rush upward in leapfrog fashion, almost running. In no time at all we are midway up the face. Now, from above, suddenly there resounds a hideous screech.

"What's that?"

"I dunno. Sounds dreadful!" We search the heavens.

"There!" In the deep-violet twilight of inner space we see it.

"Oh my God, it's huge!" With an immense wingspan of more than thirty feet, this bird takes flight from the needlelike summit, then drifts slowly down toward us. Its huge body is entirely black except for a helmet of white feathers. Now from two thousand feet above it tucks its wings.

"Rob!" yells Harley. "I think it's a lammergeier."

"It's diving at us. Harley, watch out!"

We scurry for shelter like rabbits caught out on a roadway. There is none. We are totally exposed. Cowering, we hug the ice surface beneath our packs as it screeches by. Its great leathery talons clamp down upon Harley's pack. "Rob, help me," he screams in terror. It shears the pack from his back and carries it aloft.

"We've got to get out of here—now!"

"Oh no! Here it comes again!" I scream as it begins another dive. As it swarms down upon us, I lurch leftward to escape its grasp. By inches it misses me. But it snags my boot! In a split second the talons clamp down and snap it from my body. "My foot," I scream, staring down at the stump. It is bloodless. "Oh, Harley, he's taken my foot!"

Harley watches the bird rise up, still clutching my foot, until it disappears in the blackness beyond the mountain. "He's gone, he's gone," yells Harley happily. "C'mon, we can still make the summit."

"Harley, my foot. It's gone."

"Forget it, Rob. C'mon, let's go."

"Rob, Rob. Come and eat."

"OK, Mom. Be there in just a minute."

Da-ding, da-ding, da-ding da-ding, da-ding. "Come, children, recess is over. Back to the classroom." *Da-ding da-ding, da-ding, da-ding.*

*   *   *

The clatter of metal awakens me. *"Habari-chai!"*

I open my eyes to see a small, plump black woman dressed in white in the center of the room. In her hand she holds a metal pitcher, and before her stands a battered table-height dolly with a huge five-gallon pot resting upon it. Languidly she fills the pitcher from the vat and then methodically doles out its steaming brown watery contents around the room into patients' outstretched cups. I haven't the faintest idea what *chai* is, but I suspect from its brown color it must be tea or perhaps coffee. Tea or coffee, hot or cold, it is liquid. I am so parched dry I can barely swallow now.

She finishes filling the cup of the back-tube patient beside me. I prepare to tell her I need a cup. But she turns and shuffles straight past over to the "Moslem" on the other side without giving me so much as a glance. How could she miss me? Shocked by this obvious snub, I sit stunned as she finishes her rounds and begins on seconds. My face flushes red as she prepares to push the dolly from the ward. "Excuse me," I yell at her. She spins around and looks at me for the first time. Staring straight into her murky brown eyes, I loudly and staunchly say, "I'd like a cup of tea, please," gesturing toward the large metal pot. Fifteen seconds or more she stands there motionless, staring at me as if what I said needed deciphering. Still looking me square in the eye, she lifts both shoulders up to her ears in a shrug, makes a small grimacing frown, and pushes the cart out of the room. I lie there, physically helpless, overwhelmed by frustration and anger, too hurt to react with anything but blind hatred.

Her smug, haughty attitude is not a prejudicial slap against me as a white from her as a black, but more deep-reaching. It hits me as an indignity discharged against me personally, against one human being by another human, who presently rules over me. It is frightening. Yet even this affront, this pitiless control of another's life, is not sufficient. It is necessary, or so she signifies by not even acknowledging my presence, that I realize how great a command over me she does have, even to the degree of deciding when I will and when I won't eat or drink.

As I lie on my straw mattress, tears fill my eyes. This hospital will not be the merciful liberator, the compassionate savior I hoped so many days for. Alone on the mountain with God I yearned for this place—for these people to save me, to save my leg. Now, utterly alone, I long for the mountain and God once more, to save my soul. In my desolation I implore God for deliverance. Freedom. Death.

It is a minute or more before I sense the touch of his shrunken, withered hand on my right elbow. It is the "Moslem," smiling warmly, once more repeating his head-tilting greeting. With his outstretched arm he gestures toward me, cup in hand. It is a silent offering of tea. Gratefully I nod in acceptance. Across the void between our beds our hands meet, the cup passing from one to another. This simple kind gesture is more healing than any remedy this hospital could have given me.

As afternoon smolders on toward evening, the surgical ward comes alive with people. Each bed is surrounded by clusters of adults and children, five, six, seven, eight, as many as a dozen. When Odd and Rotraut return, the noisy commotion is so loud we must almost shout over the din.

"What's going on?" I yell to Rotraut.

"What do you mean, Rob?" she says.

"All these people? What are they doing here?"

"This is African life. It is not like Europe or America. Here your family must take care of you, feed you. The hospital doesn't do it."

"But where were all these people today? Where will they go tonight now?"

"Ha!" she says, smiling. "During the day they are out working, collecting food, doing business. At night they stay here with their sick family members."

"But where?"

"Anywhere, under the bed, beside it, many times in the bed itself with the patients if disease is not too serious."

"That's incredible!"

"Oh, it's true," she says, "and this is part of our problem with you. We live in Marangu, fifty kilometers one way from KCMC Hospital here in Moshi. This hospital gives only some gruel and porridge to patients—you can't survive on it alone. You must have someone to bring you meals, to watch out for you."

Odd breaks in. "Rob, Marangu is just too far for us to take care of you properly. It would be one hundred kilometers each trip and at least three a day, which we can't manage."

Continues Rotraut, "We must find someone nearby to look after you."

"I'm sorry to trouble you. If only Harley—"

"Rob, don't be ridiculous, it's no trouble. We will have someone."

Odd and Rotraut depart for their long trip back to Marangu.

Later the same small squat Bantu who earlier in the day gave out tea returns once more to the ward. *"Habari-ndizi na nyama,"* she mumbles as she hauls her cart to the center of the room. Into the towering stack of porridge bowls next to her five-gallon pot she begins doling out great ladlefuls of yellow slop flecked with brown.

As I later find out, this is one of the staples of the people of East Africa, made of green bananas and stewed meat parts. One after another I watch her distribute them about the ward, not only to the patients but also to their family members. She leans over the man next to me to give him his gruel, the one with the back tube, and I notice that he too is alone or almost alone. Ten paces off from his bed hunches a small black man against the wall in some sort of ill-fitting brown uniform with brass buttons. The woman also hands him a mounded bowl of food and then, as before, goes over to the Moslem on the other side of me. I try to stare her down as she passes, but she does not even hint at my existence. Into her turned back my eyes burn, wishfully hoping that any second she will explode in fiery conflagration and be reduced to ashes. She grabs her dolly and shuffles out of the ward.

I look back once more to the man in the baggy brown uniform.

In the back-tubed patient he is uninterested, yet he steadily gazes down at him. Silently, apart, they eat their gruel, never speaking. Each continuously keeps the other in his line of sight I have a strange feeling of uneasiness about these two. A fallen soldier watched over by his comrade? Unlikely, for there seems no friendship between them. A wounded enemy soldier or terrorist under guard by a member of the Tanzanian Army? Implausible, for there appears no animosity between them. Onward I theorize to amuse myself, to forget.

Under darkness a muffled quietness spreads over the ward, bodies piled upon the floor, crammed into and under the beds, crowded upon the windowsills, all seeking the solace of sleep.

In my solo journeys into the mountains I have felt extreme isolation and enjoyed it. Alone upon the summit, at one with the wind, the sky, the snow. Now, surrounded by this throng of people, I feel so alone, isolated as never before in my life. Why is it that one always feels desolation at its worst in the company of men when expectations of sharing and community go unfulfilled?

Woefully I slip into sleep. Pain attacks while I slumber, driving its dagger into my open, draining wounds. I cry softly to myself for relief, yet it steadily worsens. I need something. I need to call a nurse. This entire past afternoon I have not seen a single nurse in the ward. Looking across to the dimly lit hallway beyond the ward entrance, I see shadows of movement. As a last resort I call, "Nurse!" Several seconds later when no one approaches, I yell, "Nurse!" Again no one comes. I continue yelling, "Nurse! Nurse!" But there is no response. As my yells of "Nurse!" turn into howls of "*N-U-R-S-E*" as loud as I can possibly scream, some of the other patients in the ward automatically join in with me, giving my pleading chorus added emphasis and volume. "NURSEY!" "NURSEY!" "NURSEY!" we shout at the top of our lungs over and over again. Finally a huge figure waddles into the ward. Instantly the chorus stops. Silence reigns. In sharp shrills of Swahili she delivers a biting rebuke that can only be a scolding. She hones in on my small light as if it were a beacon.

Beside my bed she says gruffly, *"Unastkia maumivu?"*

"Please, I need some painkiller for my leg!"

"Wusda matta? Wha u won?" she grumbles.

"It hurts. I need some pain medication. A pill, a shot, something."

Later—thirty minutes? an hour?—she returns, syringe in hand. Roughly she sinks the jab of morphine into my left arm, squeezing forth the precious liquid relief. As she exits the ward she turns and gives one more resounding contemptuous burst of Swahili to us all.

The narcotic quickly takes effect, deadening the pain. Fitfully I ease off.

Ring-ring . . . ring-ring . . . ring-ring . . . ring-ring . . . ring-ring . . . ring-ring.

Not again! The phone outside the ward begins anew. Since my arrival at KCMC this ringing has continued almost unceasingly, at all hours of the day and night.

No one answers it. I have reread the same passage five times. Trying my best to blot out the ringing, I return to my book.

"All right, you bitch, the game's over," shouted D'Ambrosio, coming down the hall at a walk. He knew he had her cornered and that it would hurt to run.

Inside the anatomy hall, Susan paused for a moment, trying to recall the layout in the faint light. Then she bolted the door behind her. . . .

The freezer was at least ten feet wide and thirty feet deep. Susan remembered all too clearly . . . cadavers stored here for dissection . . . after embalming, they were hung up with tongs hooked into external ear canals. . . . The bodies were stiff, naked, misshapen; most were the color of pale marble. The females were mixed with the males, the Catholics with the Jews, the whites with the blacks in the equality of death. . . .

D'Ambrosio gasped, not even feeling the pain from his broken rib. He was staring at a cadaver. The head was dissected free of skin, the teeth and eyes were bared. The hair had been undermined and folded back like a pelt. The front of the chest was gone, as was the front of the abdomen. The organs, which had been removed, were piled back into the opened body haphazardly. . . .

He opened the freezer door and again fell back in horror. The hanging bodies appeared like an army of ghouls. . . .

"Come on, Sweetheart. Don't make me search this place."

"Rob!"

I look up. "Odd, Rotraut."

"How do you feel? Did you sleep OK?"

"Eventually, after some morphine, I got a little. But that damn phone. It rings endlessly—hours. No one answers it."

"Rob," Odd says, smiling, "this is Africa. If they answer the phone, it might mean more work."

"Rob," says Rotraut, "I have someone I want you to meet. This is Karen Yoder." I follow her gesturing hand over her shoulder and for the first time see Karen standing there. Her short straight light-brown hair sweeps gently back from her classic Renoir face.

"Hi, Karen, how are you?"

"Fine!" she says in a soft, flowing voice. "The question is, *how* are *you?*"

"Well, not so great just lately."

"I can understand why." She smiles weakly. She says nothing about my leg, although I can see that the mere sight of it brings signs of disquiet to her face, worry to her eyes. Her revulsion, though well hidden beneath the veil of concern, is clear. It reminds me of the disgusting sight and smell this rotting limb presents to people. I have long since forgotten it could be any other way.

Odd tries at lightening the mood. "Rob, what are you reading?"

"A book called *Coma*."

"Oh, my God, Rob," says Karen, "how can you read that here?"

"Why?" says Rotraut. "We will bring something else, better for you!"

"Isn't it terrible frightening," says Odd, "in this place?"

In contrast to their sentiments, I have found that *Coma* stirs no fear or anxiety within me. I delved into Robin Cook's story to fill the hours, to distract me from the endless waves of pain and heat. In my longing for escape, I sank into *Coma*, body and mind, totally absorbed by it. Yet it is more than escape. Over the last days I have come to realize just how extreme life can be. Still caught up in my own struggle for survival, I relish this involvement in the terror of someone else and her struggle against the odds. The wild plot of the novel seems all too real. In the end *Coma* is as much a vivid reality to me as the reality of KCMC.

Now, as the Eliassens depart, the remainder of the Yoder family arrives. Keith leads the way, carrying a large wicker basket, followed closely behind by David, John, Ben, and a little daughter. With first looks, Keith gives the impression of grave severity, with his sharp features and thick black hair and beard. Yet, as soon as he speaks, I see he is very easygoing. His soft-spoken Midwestern twang and relaxed, low-key personality remind me of the actor Jimmy Stewart. The boys, from eight to twelve years old, already are as large as some of the Bantus in the ward. It is a striking image to see these three blond all-American freckled towheads here amidst the wilds of darkest Africa. To and fro they run about the surgical ward, happily gesticulating and jabbering away in Swahili with the patients. Keith Yoder, a missionary dentist, brought his family from Goshen, Indiana, to Tanzania five years earlier. The boys and daughter, Sarah, have very much grown up in Africa, in many ways like Africans. Yet there will always be differences. There have to be. From the very seeds of origin through upbringing, life-style, even spiritual beliefs, there runs a thread that parts the Yoders from the natives.

They say it is for their own selfish reasons they came to Tanzania—"sheer dissatisfaction and boredom with the American way of life." Perhaps, but I do not think they are being totally honest with me or themselves. One does not go into the jungles of Tanzania in search of the "good life." Something, some higher, more divine intent, brought them here. This is the greatest difference I see between the Tanzanians and the Yoders. If the roles were reversed, how much help could the Yoders expect from these people?

In the coming months they will leave Tanzania permanently and, with some reluctance, return to the United States of America. As Americans, Keith and Karen feel they have an obligation to their children in these formative years to expose them to the American way of life and instill in them some of the ideals and mores associated with citizenship in the United States before it may be too late. The thought of these youngsters adopting the attitude toward life and death that permeates the Bantu way of life sends a shudder through me. Yet the prospect of their buying into the American way of success—with the dollar sign as its standard—is hardly more cheery. My mind jumps across the ocean to Houston and the sports convention Harley planned to attend. Could that have been the only reason he left? I cannot squelch feelings of desertion, no matter how many times I tell myself there must have been another, unknown reason for his going. I feel he has severed the bond of the rope between us as surely as if he had cut it there on the Breach Wall, casting me adrift, alone in Africa.

I know I could not survive without the Yoders and the Eliassens. They are my God-sent saviors. Their food strengthens this body, their love mends this shattered soul. For the first time in many days I feel reassured.

In my subsequent days at KCMC Hospital, tenuously I settle into the routine of African hospital life, a life I find sometimes comic, sometimes tragic, but often filled with cruelty and callousness. In my almost constant morphinized state my senses deaden to the passage of time. Minutes, hours, days, blur and merge into one, separated only by the visits of the Yoders and the Eliassens, or by specific, sometimes startling incidents that transpire in the ward.

Each morning opens the same: *"Habari za asabuhi!"* ("What is the news of this day!") A young Bantu girl dressed in pink and white, a nurse trainee, greets us as she distributes bedpans, urinals, and toilet paper to us. Every morning I accept a stainless-steel urinal from her. Always it reeks that same rancid smell of stale, soured urine. Sometimes it is still partly full from yesterday's usage.

Every morning when she attempts to hand me a metal bedpan I say, "I don't have to go just now, but leave it and I'll use it later after I eat."

Always she says only, "No!" Her face darkens as she turns and scurries out of the ward. In a moment she returns with the huge head floor nurse dressed in blue.

"Wasammatta?" the nurse growls at me, gesturing toward the bedpan, whose interior is besmudged with smears of stool and wet dollops of used toilet paper.

"I can't go before I eat. Just leave it, I'll go after breakfast."

For a moment she smiles at our standoff, then, brows creasing, she grows serious. "Ya down go no ya down go!" tilting forward her hefty head as a sign of punctuation—period.

An explosive howling from across the room disrupts our little parley, and all eyes turn to look at the source. There upon a stainless-steel bedpan sits, stark naked, the withered ancient Masai. With each push he howls as he bears down in vain, struggling with his balky bowels. Almost immediately, upon seeing him, the two nurses beside me break out into loud, hysterical laughter. Going over to his side, they playfully tickle him, poking him in the ribs till he also is giggling. Soon the entire ward is rolling about in waves of laughter at this poor man's plight, a proud Masai warrior losing the battle of the bedpan to a Bantu woman.

Nine A.M. is medication time. The small crash cart is dragged into the ward by two candy-striped nurse trainees. From the disheveled jumble of bottles, jugs, and paper cups on the small cart top they dole out the various pills and medicines to the patients. This is usually done not without a fair amount of confusion. It is a common sight to see pills prescribed and given to a patient only to have a nurse trainee minutes later snatch them from his grasp just as he is about to swallow them, replacing them with others.

During this time each day, head nurse "Big Blue" enters the ward, huge wad of cotton in one hand, a fistful of syringes in the other. Beside my bed she reaches out for my arm. In her hand is undoubtedly one of the largest syringes I have ever seen. The barrel is almost an inch across, and it is filled three-quarters full with thick white penicillin. "Cumon, gimmee ya 'rm." Instinctively I recoil, withdrawing my arm. "Cumon!"

"What? You're not going to put all that in my arm!" She nods her head in jovial affirmation. "You're crazy! I'm not going to let you do it."

Reaching down, she taps the top of my thigh and repeats, "Cumon!"

"No way! It's too much at one time—anywhere."

She lashes forth, "Stoppat-no!" I sense her anger rising, "Yu vhama git dis zot umy hou. Dis orda fea dokka e-zak-sun."

We stare at each other, immovable, at seemingly interminable loggerheads. Finally she cedes to my one steadfast condition, the injection shall be distributed over four areas, my two arms and my two thighs. With each jab of the needle I wince as the white, gluey penicillin swells beneath my skin into a hard lump within my muscle tissue. All the while she giggles and laughs.

Every face becomes suspect as a possible enemy, as another messenger of pain. Do they revel in my discomfort because I'm white? Do they neglect me out of spite? I soon see this is not the case at all. Their callousness toward me simply reflects their primitive life-style, an existence where life is cheap, death a daily companion. There is no respect for any life but one's own. To survive here one must look out for number one, fighting for one's own needs and wants. No one else will. From birth to death it is an existence centered solely upon self-preservation. To survive is to succeed.

Each morning doctors' rounds come in the surgical ward between 10 and 10:30 A.M. The overabundance of patients at KCMC and the general lack of medical personnel necessitate that the doctor on call each morning make rounds on all the patients. Consequently, out of all the cases he will review each day, very few will be his own. Ward to ward he goes, bed to bed, demurely smiling, nodding attentively over each chart, concerning patients about whom he knows nothing and for whom he can or will do nothing. Yet I can see it does have a great effect of appeasement upon my fellow ward mates as they lie back rested, reassured, after "the doctor" has seen them.

Dr. Isaakson has thus far barely managed to save my leg by boring holes through my ankle for synovial drains. Yet his act alone is not sufficient. It is necessary that a steady and constant supply of fluid pass through the hoses to flush out the poison. This is done by hanging a giant IV bottle above the foot of my bed and draining it into the tubes. The volume of flow is controlled by a small crimping valve on the tube below the bottle. Once it is empty the supply is replenished with a new bottle and the process repeated once more. Several times I hear Dr. Isaakson reiterate to the ward nurses the importance of maintaining constant, steady flow. He stresses to them in the simplest of terms—the swifter and greater the volume of the fluid passing through the ankle, the more effective the treatment will be, thus the better chances of saving the leg. Yet his words stay in their minds no longer than his presence before their eyes. The large IV bottle is perched upon a tall, slender strand of steel almost four feet above my bed to achieve the proper gravity feed. As the pole is unadjustable and the bottle beyond reach, the nurses must climb upon a stool or, as is usual, my mattress, for each change.

The first day they soon tire of this relentless procedure, deeming it too much effort. Although they cannot simply stop the procedure Dr. Isaakson has ordered, their solution is to tighten down the crimping valve so as to drastically reduce the flow, thereby reducing greatly the number of bottles needing to be changed. Every opportunity, when certain I am not being watched, I take retaliatory measures, as necessary for my own self-preservation. Leaning forward, keeping an ever-watchful eye on the door of the ward, I stretch upward to the crimping valve, just within reach, and open it full. Later, bottle empty, I reclose it and begin calling for another bottle. Over a number of bottles this procedure works, until the nurses begin to realize there are as many bottle changes, as before, if not more. At first they suspect a broken valve, yet, in typical fashion, neglect to change it or even examine it closely. Thus I keep at my covert maneuvers, in fact, several days with success. But one morning I am caught fiddling with the valve by the head nurse. The war between us begins in earnest. Nurses—the enemy. As determined as they are not to be disturbed by the efforts of the bottle changing, I am more determined to keep my leg. Toward the end they threaten to delay bottle changes to stop my persistence and finally even withhold several treatments entirely. Yet, with every bottle hung I make certain the proper flow registers. After days of battle it appears I shall lose this war. "Big Blue" enters the ward with a. smug, self-satisfied grin on her face, and IV pole in hand. She changes the long IV pole on my bed to an even longer one—the IV bottle is now mere inches from the ceiling. The crimping valve is beyond my reach.

With each passing day the anger grows within me. Yet, as great as the indignities of this hospital may be, and daily they increase, certainly they are no worse than the infirmities that confine us here. They are the true inequities.

Others are not nearly so fortunate as I, in particular the ancient

Masai across from me, with the fractured knee. He always seems to receive the worst of it. The Masai are a unique, elite tribe in Africa, different from other tribes in more than just looks. Most tribes readily and willingly have adapted themselves to the rapid march of progress the white man has brought to Africa. They eagerly adopt this new life-style, casting aside centuries of ritual, belief, and custom for transistor radios, Mars bars, and whiskey. The Masai are a definite exception. They have clung to their ancient way of life as nomadic herders, their cattle still their most esteemed possession. They are totally dependent upon the herd for supplying necessities, blood and milk for food, skins and fur for shelter and clothing. Nothing is useless, nothing wasted, nothing more is needed. Around the herd revolve their lives. These striking differences have often brought down upon the Masai the animosity of other tribes. This is the only reason I can find for the Bantu nurses' enduring ill-treatment of this old one. For days on end they ignore the bandages on his knee until the noxious odor smothers the ward. When they finally do strip them off, always they are sopping, green with sepsis. Because of the neglect, his wound has become severely infected, covered by maggots. For no apparent reason the nurses take every opportunity to further torment him. With great delight, in twos and threes, they gather about his knee, swollen almost double in size, and press down upon it, giggling as he howls in pain. Almost as if in lighthearted competition they take turns squeezing billows of pus from his wound onto the mattress. The indignities never cease. Yet, ever silent, never does he utter a word against them.

During my hospital stay, daily I watch this old Masai worsen, weaken. His eyes lose their brilliance. He stops eating. Soon he barely moves. One morning he is sheeted and removed from the ward. In the end they have won, breaking him bodily. But in doing so they set his spirit free to roam the plains of Masailand for eternity.

Under the stifled stillness of afternoon, drowsily I look up. Dr. Isaakson stands at the foot of my bed, somber and stone-faced as ever. A stab of anxiety runs through me.

"Rob, we have done all that we can for you. Because of the nature of your infection, you are in need of special treatment and medications unavailable here." Pause. "I shall discharge you to go home."

Home? *Home!* I can't believe my ears. Never again did I think I would hear such wonderful words.

"There is a flight Sunday. We have been in contact with your family and they have paid for medical seating arrangements with British Airways, for assistance the entire journey home. This will assure that your leg will be kept elevated at all times." He tells me that Odd has already brought my medical travel release to the British Airways office to allow me to travel and that all is in order. I will be transported to the airport by stretcher and lifted aboard. He reemphasizes, "You must keep your foot up at all times. I will give no crutches, to assure this. Again, you must not let your leg hang down or you will lose it."

From the dark confines of KCMC at last I escape. I am delivered from it into the brilliant sunshine. Tears of joy stream down my cheeks as I squint back at the overpowering yellow light, breathing in the clean fresh air.

Arriving at the Kilimanjaro International Airport, we are dismayed to find that they have no record of any medical arrangements having been made. While I lie outside the terminal under a date palm in the scorching heat, Odd tries to explain to the BA personnel that there has been some sort of oversight. All has been totally paid for in advance from the States. He keeps insisting that they check. His pleas fall on deaf ears, unregistered in the blank complacent faces, unacknowledged save for head nods, shoulder shrugs, and occasional finger thrusts at the silent Telex machine. "No word, no word." The plane is delayed many hours, and while we wait he keeps trying, but to no avail. When we find that the plane is not sold out, we decide I should use my original return ticket and prop my leg up on an adjacent seat. Once I get to London, all will be straightened out.

The runway shimmers violently, full of round puddled mirages in the searing 112-degree heat of midafternoon. The blazing inferno can be felt even within the air-conditioned cabin of the jet as streams of sweat soak my cotton shirt and trousers. Looking out my small oval window for some sign of movement and relief, I gaze by chance down at the runway. There two large translucent scorpions lie locked in mortal combat. Over and over they twist and turn, each struggling to gain the upper hand. Repeatedly lashing out, they drive home their venomous tail stingers into each other. The plane revs its engines and slowly begins taxiing to the runway. Fatally wounded, the two scorpions slip from my view, still entwined, each having only the other in the throes of death.

Slowly at first the Tri-star rolls forward, then, engines beginning to strain, it moves faster, and faster, and faster, until airborne. Angling sharply upward, it clears the coffee and banana shambas and streaks northward—home. Toward Liberty Ledge. My spirit soars.

Out of my window to the east the white countenance of Kilimanjaro stands out abruptly amidst the green jungles. At this altitude I am face to face with the mountain. The stark contrast, white and green, is striking. I realize it is no more so than the Africa I have seen, experienced—a land of contrasts. Ice and sun; cold and heat; cruelty and kindness; machine guns and banana shambas; confidence and despair; then and now; unscathed vitality and blighted immobility; Harley and Odd; expectation and reality.

XIII

I reach out to my sister Mercy
The computer says I'm not here at all
Her response is only heartless cursing
Duty first is the corporate call

In the early-morning hours British Airways Flight 090 arrives in London. One of the cabin crew radios for the medivan, which transports me to the Heathrow Medical Unit. I am happy to see Joe Monahan, a friend who has come out from London after hearing the news from my family. Within the unit the nurse in charge, Sister A. Didymus, insists she has no listing of an immobile person on her computer! I assure her my family has paid for the necessary transportation arrangements, from the States. I tell her that, although I may not be listed on her computer, still I lie before her now, a reality. I need help.

Joe steps in and insists that he has spoken to my mother. "All special arrangements have been paid for."

Sister Didymus snaps back, "I don't think we can take Mum's word for it!" She remains unsympathetic. Without a listing on her computer, I do not exist. It is as if compassion has been programmed out of her for the sake of efficiency.

Joe tries to direct her attention to the situation at hand, but she begins firing questions at me. She repeats in shock and abhorrence each response I give. How did I manage from Africa, she wonders, without medical arrangements, without crutches, without special seating accommodation?

"By keeping my leg up on an adjacent seat!"

She becomes furious. That is strictly against all International Air Transportation Association rules and regulations.

I try to explain that the next direct flight from Kilimanjaro was seven days later and that as a paramedic I understood the seriousness of my condition—I was literally trying to save my leg.

What about my water, how did I relieve my bladder on such a long journey?

"The doctor gave me a pee bottle which I used shielded beneath a blanket!"

Her face registers utter disgust. "What would have happened if your bowels had opened?" she acidly demands. "I can well imagine!" she answers, not awaiting my reply. She makes it clear that her duty first and foremost is to protect the interests of BA and the rights of respectable paying passengers. Amused, I think to myself, If only she had seen me two days ago—before Rotraut and Karen had given me my first bath in over a month.

She continues smugly that I may have gotten this far but she herself will see to it I'll get no farther unless she receives official word that I have prepaid arrangements. She says that I cannot spend the night at the Heathrow Medical Unit and that BA can be of no assistance transporting me elsewhere. If need be they will put me out on the street till morning. The jolly image of Robert Morley comes to mind, in bowler hat and pinstriped suit, saying, "British Airways. We'll take good care of you."

Out into the drizzling night Joe wheels me, away from the medical unit. I think back to Africa, to the hospital. Initially I was shocked at the people's attitude toward life and death. I was an alien in their world. A harsh, cruel world. I tried to understand and perhaps even accept the fatalism of their outlook on life. But not here. This is my world, refined, developed, civilized. Have we come full circle?

XIV

You tell me that it's all my fault
Divided we stand
Together we fall

It is a cold, steel-gray afternoon the day I arrive back in Boston from Africa. The high overcast sky is reminiscent of that boyhood day on Mount Osceola long ago. After a tearful reunion with my family at Logan Airport's Volpe Terminal, I am swept off to Emerson Hospital's special-care unit. There, over the following weeks, a steady stream of doctors come and go; the medical jargon flows forth. At times it is difficult to wade through the flood. Mostly I am too sick to care.

It is a time of uncertainty, yet promise, slight improvement; then the fetid smell returns to my foot and all seems for naught, a time when X rays eventually show that the bone is being eaten from within by anaerobic infection, when my family's optimism keeps me going, and when Pamela, my nurse on Wheeler II, becomes part of my life.

All during my hospitalization I try to keep an open mind as to Harley's actions and attitude in Africa, particularly his leaving me. There must be a good and logical reason for his doing so. In the newspaper stories and in talking with people, I do not tell the whole story, but reiterate how he saved my life. Still the doubts persist, and I often wonder why he didn't go to the radio that was so close; and as the weeks pass in my waiting for Harley to come and see me, more questions are raised than answered. During the course of my stay in the hospital, I learn from my family that Harley paid them a visit the night he returned from Africa. In dribs and drabs the details of his story that night surface, sometimes in the most peculiar ways. My sister Chris asks, "Why did your ice screw come out on the icicle?" I tell her it didn't. She is surprised. "That's not what Harley told Mom. He said you were climbing sloppy, too fast, trying to force the route. You fell, pulled out your only ice screw, and smashed feet first into the base of the icicle."

Later my mother declares how fortunate I was to have Dr. Moirer caring for me. "Undoubtedly he saved your leg and life." She is more than a little surprised when I tell her Dr. Isaakson from Sweden, not Dr. Moirer, was the physician whose skill saved my leg.

"How can this be?" she wonders, "All Harley spoke of was Dr. Moirer. Wasn't he the doctor who treated you when Harley brought you into the hospital?"

I tell her Harley never saw me at the hospital. He was gone by the time I was off the mountain.

"You mean he just got you to the hospital and then left?"

I tell her that Harley did not go back up the mountain, that he was not on the rescue. The last time I saw him was Monday morning beneath the Breach Wall at sixteen thousand feet when he went for help.

She is shocked. "Harley expressly told us he was at the hospital with you Thursday night, and he certainly gave us all the impression he was on the rescue."

The mystery thickens and I am left with more questions about Harley than I began with. I ponder the details of his visit that night to my home and his conversation with my family and Melinda, a close friend who was also present. I am all the more puzzled by the strange composite picture Harley has painted. He set a bizarrely light, carefree atmosphere that evening for the bearer of bad tidings. Melinda says he came to the house laughing and joking. His mood was expansive and buoyant. "It's not as serious as Rob imagined," Harley told them. "He's got a broken ankle." Still Mark decided to leave immediately for Africa. Harley told him pointedly not to go, everything was all set now, taken care of. It would be a waste of time, and Mark could be of no help to me. Seeing the severity of my condition now, it is incomprehensible to my family how they had been so misled.

That evening Harley talked incessantly and at length about me and himself. He said he didn't know what I was doing in Africa. I was frightened and paranoid all the time at everything. He told them I had destroyed his respect for me as a climber and that I was completely in the wrong line of work. Mountains were the last place I ought to be. He felt we should all have a long talk when I recovered to try to convince me to pursue a profession better suited to my nervous temperament. He went on to say that although I generally showed tremendous courage, one time when I was weak and whining he threatened to cut the rope and leave me there if I didn't shut up. "And I would have, too," he asserted to my family that night with conviction.

Mostly Harley talked about himself, though, his experiences in Africa and how he'd had the time of his life there. The incredible photos he'd taken of me just after the accident and then struggling on the descent would be worth a fortune to him. He would get four times his usual fee for a lecture of this adventure. Adventure. That's the word that most aptly sums up the impression Harley gave them of the Breach. And there could be no doubt now as to the hero of this adventure, for as Harley recounted, "I know there is not another person alive with both the skill and strength to get Rob safely down from the Breach Wall." On and on he rambled throughout the night, describing in detail his many exploits and successes round the world, in Dresden, California, Australia, Britain. It was almost as if he needed to reassure himself as much as them of his great ability and reputation as a climber.

At the first light of dawn, he left to the heartfelt thanks of my family for all he had done for me. For saving my life.

Several weeks after my accident on the Breach Wall, early one morning a call comes through to my hospital room. It is from the manufacturer of the sleeping bags we used in Africa. They have a picture of me taken just after the accident on the icicle. I am lying on a small ledge, and from the look on my face it is obvious I am close to shock and in severe pain. Oddly enough, just at my side lies one of their sleeping bags, its label clearly defined. It's a perfect shot, he tells me, almost as if it had been set up. They are going to purchase rights from Harley Warner for five hundred dollars; it will be used on a nationwide ad campaign. He wants to know how I like the headline "In severe Alpinism you don't always reach the top—that's when you can fall back on 29K sleeping bags." I tell him I don't. There are many things by this time I don't like.

It is strange how one becomes accustomed to an individual's inconceivable behavior. Instead of being shocking, it becomes characteristic. Since Harley has not yet been to see me, I call and ask him to please stop by. Eight weeks to the day after the accident we have our first meeting in my hospital room. I start out by thanking him for all that he's done for me in Africa. Then we rehash the whole experience. I tell him that I feel that we both made some mistakes and serious errors in judgment. We should talk about them. I feel especially bad about his condescending attitude and his deserting me. Harley matter-of-factly responds, "Rob, you know I had to get back for the sports convention; and you may well have made a lot of mistakes in Africa. I have not. I am not sorry for anything I have done and would do the exact same thing again in similar circumstances." There is nothing more to say. Harley departs. "The mountains labor," says the Latin poet, "and they bring forth a mouse."

I now realize that the Breach was not an isolated climbing accident nor merely the failure of a partnership and its unraveling. Much more, it was a disaster in human relationships. I was shortsighted in not taking Harley's full personality into account— as a given. An avalanche is not malicious unto itself, nor was

Harley. He was what he was. I had simply failed to recognize this.

Today is over. We err to think that another day will be what we wished today to be or that another person will become the one we hoped he really was.

XV

After the fall
Beyond the dream
Lies one's full identity

The grass glistens with dew this midsummer morn as I pen these thoughts to you. We are in the midst of a heat wave here at Liberty Ledge. I've escaped with my writing out-of-doors to seek relief under a sprawling pine near the house. Africa, Kilimanjaro, the events of the Breach are two years past. My leg is still with me, although it is the leg I brought home from Kili, not the one I took to her. I have a permanent limp.

In all our lives there comes a time, at least once, when our past catches us up. It can't be outrun or avoided any longer. For me this day of reckoning came upon the Breach. I knew then, while still on the Wall, that I could blame no one but myself for the accident, because of my lack of assertiveness. It would have been easy to say it was someone else's fault—he let the rope slip. But the fault was mine in not having the fortitude to stand up for my convictions. Those final days in Africa I lost my vision, that inner vision we must all have to carry on, to aspire, to be. Blinded, I returned home feeling less than a total being, bearing a concept of self as much in need of repair as my body.

Before I could begin the forward process of recovery I first had to reverse, mentally and spiritually, go back to Africa, return to the Breach. Those past days needed to be relived, rescrutinized in their minutest detail, if I was to glean some understanding of my present loss of self. A return to Africa so soon was a painful journey to make, even if only mentally. The wounds of the experience still bled. Yet time and again I took that trip. Over ten, eleven, twelve months I must have made the passage ten thousand times, awake and in my dreams, in my meditations and deliberations, in my conscience and in my subconscious. I sought out my missing parts to be whole once more. But simple knowledge of events often does not bring an overall understanding of an affair. Revelation unfolds, slowly, over time as the facts, like discrete pieces of a jigsaw puzzle, come together to create an impression. Unlike a jigsaw puzzle, we never really know when we are finished.

At this stage of my journey back from the Breach I become daily more aware of the positive aspects of the pilgrimage there. Africa has renewed in me a reverence and deep appreciation for the gift of life, for my own and for that of the English sparrow who darts overhead, or the solitary ant beneath my table, who struggles over serrated dandelion leaf with his crumb of food for the colony. It is wonderful to be alive. I see the world through different eyes today and no one more differently than I see myself. It is only in times of extreme stress that we truly define ourselves, perhaps gaining a glimmer of who we really are. Those weeks of protracted strain in Africa, the accident, the descent, the hospital—they drew out from me every reserve of strength I had. It was necessary to give all just to survive. Because of this I have a much deeper understanding and acceptance now of the great strength and resolution human beings possess.

There are no magic formulas or patents for survival. A man is a unique individual. No two alike. In an ordeal, what one man may survive, another may not. In the last throes of life one must look within himself and to God for reserves and strength. This is where success and life are to be found. In the months following my accident, everyone generally agreed that my leg could never be the same again, not after such damage. They told me I must think about the drastic change in my life-style that lay ahead.

There would be no more mountains for me. They said it was a miracle I was alive and with my leg attached besides; I should be grateful. I was and am most appreciative to be whole. Yet I could not accept their dismal prognosis so easily. I could not after Africa. The Breach had shown me where there lay faith and determination, even against the odds, there lay hope and success. Eight months after my accident I took my first unaided step. A year and a half later I returned to the mountains.

My love of mountains and climbing has not been diminished by the events on Kilimanjaro. Alpinism, the mountain world, remains my life, what I live for. Today I return to them with the enthusiasm and ardor of that small boy thirteen years ago. Though my accident has cost me the magic of youth, that supple ease of movement, that untiring vitality on the hills, still I am grateful to tread the mountains' lofty flanks, drink in the beauty of their heights in any capacity.

The Breach has altered my concept of death. I see death now not as an end of life but as a beginning of one. It marks the transition to a reality that we cannot comprehend. I do not pretend to say I know death or even understand it, but I glimpsed its shadow those final days alone on Kili. I feared it, but the fear I felt was not the imminent termination of my life but the unknown which death harbored beyond for me. In the end I came to terms with it by sifting through my life, casting away the worthless junk, saving for my kit bag only the most precious of my possessions, love, friendship, kindness, faith, family. In many ways I have come to see death's journey as the beginning of wisdom. Africa has not turned me into a callous individual who cares not if he lives or dies. On the contrary, it has elevated and honed my sense of the value in living and dying. Before the Breach, when friends died I mourned their passing. The tragedy was death having sapped their lives in the prime. I realize now the selfishness of my ways. I mourned not their deaths, but their loss to me, present and future. The camaraderie, the friendship, the sharing. They had gone, taking with them my joys, my dreams, my expectations, leaving behind an unfillable void in my life. My brush with death impresses upon me the mortality of man on this earth. I have a new sincerity and urgency with all those surrounding me. I must make the most of each encounter, each meeting. Who knows if it is to be our last?

I don't often talk of my companion watcher these days. He is a creature out of place here, misunderstood. After the Breach when I first spoke of him to people, they reacted quite predictably: "What an imagination!" "Your fever had you hallucinating." At first I persisted in my stand: "He was real. There in the flesh or at least in some concrete form I could see." Later I left him out altogether. It was easier than trying to define or defend him to people who could not understand. Now I know this and say this to you: He *was* there and as real as you or I. I do not know to this day his purpose, but I sense that it was good. Was he God's messenger, there to ease death's journey for me, or was he part of the spirit in humankind that says live? I do not know. Perhaps both.

The passage of time has revealed to me that an experience such as the Breach, painful as it may be, offers a wealth of insight and wisdom if one doesn't get too hung up on the "if onlys." One must recognize mistakes and poor judgment in order to profit by them and realign oneself or one is doomed to repeat them in the future. Within every man there is a creature against whom he must struggle in order to rise up, to improve himself. Two years ago I went off to climb the Breach Wall. I failed. Yet in failing I found myself, clearly defining that creature I was and that which I sought to be. If I had succeeded upon the Breach it would have been just another peak. Yet, now I have overcome an adversary far greater than any mountain.

Throughout this whole affair and afterward, events have unfolded, blossomed, then faded. Always I have had the feeling that the battle of the Breach would soon be over, just a memory. I leave you now, but the Breach remains.

Rob Taylor, who conquered a childhood fear of heights to become an avid climber of New Hampshire's White Mountains by age eleven, is a professional alpinist, naturalist, photographer, and free-lance writer. Attaining mountain expertise in Scotland under Hamish MacInnes, he has climbed throughout the world and worked in mountain rescue, avalanche control, mountain photography and cinematography for *National Geographic* and the BBC. His photographs have appeared, among other places, on the covers of *Outside* and the *New York Times Magazine*. Mr. Taylor lives in Sudbury, Massachusetts.